WANNA PLAY™

Friendship Skills for
Preschool and Elementary Grades

RUTH HERRON ROSS BETH ROBERTS-PACCHIONE

CORWIN PRESS
A SAGE Publications Company
Thousand Oaks, CA 91320

For information:

Corwin Press
A Sage Publications Company
2455 Teller Road
Thousand Oaks, California 91320
www.corwinpress.com

Sage Publications Ltd.
1 Oliver's Yard
55 City Road
London EC1Y 1SP
United Kingdom

Sage Publications India Pvt. Ltd.
B-42, Panchsheel Enclave
Post Box 4109
New Delhi 110 017 India

Printed in the United States of America

Library of Congress Cataloging-in-Publication Data

Ross, Ruth, 1974-
Wanna play: Friendship skills for preschool and elementary grades / Ruth Ross and Beth Roberts-Pacchione.
    p. cm.
ISBN 1-4129-2803-6 or 978-1-4129-2803-8 (cloth)
ISBN 1-4129-2804-4 or 978-1-4129-2804-5 (pbk.)
    1. Social skills—Study and teaching (Elementary) 2. Social skills in children—Study and teaching. 3. Children with disabilities. 4. Children with social disabilities.
I. Roberts-Pacchione, Beth. II. Title.
HM691.R67 2007
372.82—dc22   2006017787

This book is printed on acid-free paper.

06 07 08 09 10 9 8 7 6 5 4 3 2 1

Acquisitions Editor:	Kathleen McLane
Editorial Assistant:	Jordan Barbakow
Production Editor:	Denise Santoyo
Typesetter:	C&M Digitals (P) Ltd.
Cover Designer:	Rose Storey

Contents

Acknowledgments

First and foremost, we wish to thank our families for the love, support, and faith in us they have shown over the years. We would like to particularly thank Ron, Sarah, Kylie, Scott, and Paul for their never-ending patience. We would never have gotten this far without you.

We would also like to thank those involved in the Wanna Play program's internship for their energy and enthusiasm. Your work will touch many children for years to come, and we wish you luck in your future. Finally, we would like to thank the families we have been working with over the years. The parents and children we have had the honor to work with have taught us the true meaning of strength. We have learned more than we have taught.

Ruth Herron Ross, left, and Beth Roberts-Pacchione, right, and respective children.

About the Authors

Ruth Herron Ross, coauthor and director of the Wanna Play program and a founding director of the Exceptional Needs Foundation , received a Bachelor of Science in Education from Beaver College and a Master of Science in Special Education and Specialty Reading from St. Joseph's University. She has worked in a variety of roles such as lead teacher, math enrichment teacher, and summer camp director. That background helped develop and hone her abilities in working with teaching teams, classroom organization, and lesson planning and implementation. Herron Ross also received training in a variety of one-on-one early intervention and home programs. Her 12 years of education experiences, including her early intervention training, gave her the foundation of knowledge in childhood development, language acquisition, interactive behavior, and socialization skills that enabled her to create the Wanna Play program. She has been facilitating social-skill groups and individual sessions for children ages 3 through 15 years for the past 8 years at the Pennsylvania location of the Wanna play program.

Beth Roberts-Pacchione is coauthor and codirector of the Wanna Play program and cofounder of the Exceptional Needs Foundation. Beth will receive her Master of Arts degree in Counseling Psychology at Eastern University in the spring of 2007 and will then continue the process to become a licensed counselor in Pennsylvania. After her daughter was diagnosed with global developmental delay and autistic tendencies, she was uncertain about how to best help her. She decided to both receive training in and administer a home-based program, called Son-Rise, to treat these disorders. She also researched, tested, and utilized many different alternative therapies, dietary interventions, and behavioral approaches before creating the Exceptional Needs Foundation in 2001. Roberts-Pacchione has also been trained in Floortime and Interactive Metronome and has worked in Applied Behavior Analysis programs. For the past 8 years at the Pennsylvania location of the Wanna Play program, she has facilitated social-skill groups and individual sessions for children ages 3 through 15 years. She is now beginning to counsel adults to provide therapeutic support to parents whose children have been diagnosed with special needs.

Introduction

Welcome to the Wanna Play Program

This program is based on our experience working with children on their social development. We have developed and applied this curriculum over a number of years and observed its success. This curriculum can be used by *anyone* who is helping children develop their friendship skills. Because of the wide range of activities provided, it can be tailored to many different children's needs.

Based on our experience, a child with social challenges does not learn the skills necessary for successful interaction by observing typically developing peers in the classroom. More direct instruction on how to socially interact is needed in order for them to learn these abstract skills. A child does not need to have a diagnosis in order to have challenges in developing social skills. We provide training to teachers and professionals and instruction to children in a child-centered curriculum to encourage success in all areas of social interaction.

The program helps children develop basic social skills through lessons, games, and activities in group or one-on-one settings. It offers new and varied experiences that provide children the opportunity to expand their imaginations, broaden their play activities, and strengthen their social appropriateness. The primary focus of the curriculum is on pre-kindergarten to early elementary–aged children. However, it can also easily be adapted for use with preschool children.

We have been successfully using our education, personal experience, and passion in children's social development for 6 years. We found that children were not using the social skills they had learned in school and community settings. There were few programs dealing with socialization that accommodated children on many different interactive levels. We have directed social groups in our Pennsylvania location as well as run groups and trained professionals in schools and other therapeutic environments. The curriculum that we developed, the Wanna Play program, is flexible and easily personalized for the specific needs of each child. It has been made ready for publication so that it can reach a wider audience.

There is a wide audience who would benefit from utilizing this program and incorporating the lessons and activities into their work with children. Educators working with children in school settings, including teachers, both special and regular education; school psychologists; and school counselors, can incorporate the curriculum by using the lessons with individual children, small groups, or whole classrooms. Therapy professionals whose area of specialization impacts social development, such as occupational therapists, speech therapists, and behavior specialists, can also utilize the program and use it with their clients. Mental health professionals including psychologists, psychiatrists, and social workers can use the lessons as part of their therapy sessions that concentrate on the development of social awareness. Caregivers including parents, child care providers, and in-home support staff who are concentrating on their children's social development can use the program, particularly those with special needs children who have home therapy programs.

The underlying intention of all of the attitudinal approach strategies contained in this program is to be in touch with our own positive playfulness. We need to be aware of outside influences that alter our affect. When we are working on something as important as children's social development, the time spent working on our own attitude is as vital as the time spent instructing the children. We need to make sure that the children's time is their time, and that we put our own concerns aside during this time. Anyone who is reading this curriculum is doing so because he or she loves children and wants to help them. Enjoy what you are giving them, enjoy what they are giving you, and enjoy seeing the benefits of both your efforts.

A universally accepted belief in education, therapy, and any developmental discipline for children is that modeling skills and behaviors is the best way for children to internalize them. Therefore we say to you, above all, *have fun!*

Guidelines for Curriculum Success

You will not be successful using this curriculum unless you read this section. This is the only time you will read a negative statement in this book. The true success of this program begins with the reading of this section to fully understand the philosophy behind the curriculum and for the children to truly learn the social concepts taught. The purpose of this section is to give the facilitator an overview of the key concepts and to support him or her in understanding the importance of these concepts to enhance the child's success. In this section, we will explain the different parts of each unit and how to apply the lessons.

ATTITUDE

Your *affect* has a powerful *effect* on the development of social behavior. The attitude we adopt directly impacts a child's desire to make true interaction. In various trainings that we attend, we have noticed how some adults who work with children may have stern or serious affects. If we wish children to engage in and initiate interaction, we need to project a positive affect and be an engaging person. Modeling the behaviors that we want the children to use is the most effective way for them to learn those behaviors.

Listening to and really seeing the child is the best way to find the keys for helping develop social ability. We have developed this program based on a child-centered model of teaching so we can choose and adapt activities and games to suit the child's interest. Children are egocentric beings and do things according to how it benefits them. Therefore, it is important to present suggestions and strategies in a way that the child will see how the skill benefits him or her. Children do not develop appropriate social skills because it makes others happy. They adopt appropriate social behavior because over time they learn that those behaviors get them what they want.

Children will develop the affects they observe, so be mindful of what you are thinking and feeling when introducing social concepts. A positive attitude does not mean that you need to be upbeat at all times. You can be firm with children and even discipline them and still have a positive affect, as you

3

will see in the discussion of managing behavior later on in this section. It is more about internalizing a calm affect and having a "can do" attitude. Part of this involves being nonjudgmental about the behavior that a child may choose. We do not know why a child will choose a particular behavior, but we should not assume he or she is being "bad" or disrespectful. Instead, these behaviors are opportunities for us to help the child to see the benefit of choosing a positive affect like the one we have been portraying.

What we have found to be successful is to check in with others regarding how we are feeling about a particular incident or child. If we feel overwhelmed, frustrated, or just fed up with a cretin child's behavior, then it is our responsibility to re-center ourselves and find a new, proactive way of approaching the situation. Create a support system of people who focus on finding the solution rather than reliving the problem. Remember the mantra that there is always a solution to better help the child.

EYE CONTACT

Eye contact is an essential tool to successfully negotiate our social world. This skill is necessary in classroom settings for children to be able to develop concepts, comprehend information, and stay on topic when communicating with others. In social settings with adults and peers, eye contact skills help children to develop appropriate understanding of facial expression, reciprocal social communication, and the ability to stay calm and focused in a conflict situation.

In educational settings, the common assumption is that eye contact is not crucial for children to learn. Children with very poor eye contact have been observed using some skills and retaining a little of the information that was introduced when they were not making eye contact. However, it has been our experience that children do not retain all the information they need for success in social and school settings.

When a child with poor eye contact interacts with adults and peers, the inability to make eye contact impacts both the child's development of social skills and how others perceive the child's social abilities. The complexity of reciprocal interaction is a combination of learned concrete skill and abstract nonverbal behaviors. These two facets of social interaction require the use of both concrete concepts and honed observational abilities. Without sustainable frequency and duration of eye contact, children cannot learn social concepts and are not able to observe their surroundings. This results in partially developed and poorly formed social skills. Many people misinterpret poor eye contact and make negative judgments about children with disabilities or challenges. Children are identified as guilty, aloof, or disrespectful if they have poor eye contact as they get into the later elementary grades. By concentrating on eye contact now, children will be able to present themselves and express their needs in a positive way as they get older.

This is why we have dedicated an entire unit to strengthening eye contact and building the concept that sustainable eye contact is vital for successful social interaction. We also put a strong focus on the development of eye contact throughout the rest of the curriculum so children will understand that it is a skill to be used consistently. The earlier we make eye contact a priority in the social development of a child, the more success they will have as they get older.

The unit on eye contact teaches how and why we use this skill. After teaching this unit, we need to be consistent in using its strategies to help children develop eye contact throughout all of their daily interactions. We feel the following techniques are the most effective and the easiest to implement at home and in school. For overall curriculum success, utilize the suggestion listed in the Generalization and Consistency section of each lesson. These strategies should be used on a daily basis.

ASKING LEADING QUESTIONS

Leading questions are a useful teaching tool in many situations. This curriculum uses leading questions in the introduction section of each lesson. The purpose of the questions is to help the children understand the abstract concepts that will be a foundation for the activities in the lesson. Using questions and cues directs the children to formulate answers based on their own experiences. This helps the children to internalize the concept and generalize it back into a social setting. Use leading questions when developing concept maps and brainstorming lists.

Remember these things when forming your leading questions:

- Use open-ended questions and avoid "yes or no" questions.
- Use "wh" questions, starting with what and where, to help children develop concrete concepts. When asking why questions, use additional clues and specific situations to keep children on topic and encourage diverse answers.
- Use pictures and suggestions from children's immediate personal experience, especially with early readers.
- Give clues from past lessons.

WAIT TIME

The term "wait time" refers to our need to wait and give children enough time to answer. Often, if we repeat a question or direction too quickly, it will interrupt a child who is trying to process the information that has just been given. Make sure the children are given enough time to answer questions and respond to what you are asking them. We suggest that you restate the question or even repeat it after waiting a short amount of time.

Also, this is a good time to see if writing the directions down and allowing the child time to read them may help him or her process the information. Practice waiting twice your usual amount of time for the children to answer so they have more opportunity to process the first statement before you give them another to deal with.

LEARNING THROUGH FREE PLAY

The Wanna Play program begins with a child-centered philosophy and offers a curriculum to teach young children that playing is fun. Playing with friends is difficult for many children for a variety of reasons. We teach children the positive phrases and skills necessary to be successful in play scenarios. We also believe that it is best to teach and show children these strategies while they are playing.

Facilitated free play is beneficial to children for many reasons. It allows learning to occur based on something they are interested in. Also, they can immediately see the benefit of using the strategies we are teaching. All sessions will be more successful if at least part of the time is used for facilitated free play to show children how much fun it can be to play with others if they use the skills we helped them learn. There is a tendency to think that for children to be learning and developing socialization, they need to always do structured activities or worksheets. As teachers and facilitators, we should remember that free play time allows children to practice and generalize the skills they have learned in the lessons. Our role in this free play is to be active observers and facilitators so that the children are constantly in a socially supportive environment, even though it is open-ended play. The key to success in this process is knowing when to stand back and observe and when to interact and facilitate.

We use a technique we call "gorilla facilitation." The facilitator stands back, actively observing the children's interactive play and looking for opportunities to prompt social language, suggest an effective play skill, and expand play themes and diversity. This active observing also allows us to keep watch for those children who choose exclusive play over interaction and look for opportunities to redirect them toward interaction with their peers. These are the cues that teachers and facilitators should look for as opportunities to facilitate and help the children:

- Simple, exclusive, or repetitious play
- Conflict situations such as grabbing behaviors
- Inappropriate language or misused phrases

As the interactive facilitators, we need to keep aware of the intention of the free play situations. We can run the risk of "over-facilitation" during free play and not give the children the opportunity to try the skills we have introduced. Over-facilitation can happen when we are watching children attempting to use new skills on their own and we move in too soon to help.

With each of the cues we have suggested, first watch and see if the children self-correct or attempt a different strategy when interacting before moving in to offer new techniques.

During these free plays, the focus should also be on the interaction of the children. The introduction of a new game and the teaching of new play bring the focus back to the adult and take time away from the children's interaction. We suggest that preparation time be spent before the free play to learn new games or activities and help children to prepare for the play.

MANAGING BEHAVIOR

We have already discussed the importance of a positive attitude when working with children. It is just as important to discuss the affect and attitude of the children we are working with and how we can help them to maintain appropriate behavior. In most situations, when a child is using inappropriate behaviors, there is a sensory solution that will help them to re-center and cope with the situation. Children also use learned inappropriate behaviors and need to be taught the appropriate ways to interact, seek attention, and get what they want. Children can implement many different behaviors to communicate their wants and needs. Some of the options they may try to use include negative behaviors such as crying, tantrums, attempting to hurt feelings, and using emotional manipulation such as eliciting pity or guilt. It is important to try to react the same way to all of these behaviors.

In every situation involving inappropriate behavior, the first thing that needs to be done is to wait for the child to calm down before introducing solutions or new behaviors to the child. We suggest a consistent reaction to minimize negative behavior. Assess the situation. If there is a possibility of negotiation, then do it before the negative behavior begins. When a child is still not getting what he or she wants, suggest different options such as trades, deals, and bargains such as sharing and picking something new. If you make deals and bargains, be sure to hold the child to his or her part of the deal. Here are a few possible options:

- **Trades**—Someone has something you want; find something the other child might be willing to trade you for it.
- **Deals**—Make a deal so both people get what they want (e.g., you use it for 5 minutes, then I use it for 5 minutes).
- **Share**—We take turns using it (this involves working on waiting, asking with sweet words, and using something else while waiting).
- **Pick New**—Find a new cool thing to play with.

In certain situations, there is no room for negotiation. In that case, let the child know that the situation is not going to change. If the child continues to use negative behaviors, tell the child that he or she has a choice of complying now or during his or her own time. Be specific about what his or her time is (e.g., "You can clean your room now or after dinner at TV time. It is your choice, but your room needs to be cleaned.").

SENSORY SUPPORT

In our work, we have found much success in incorporating sensory support with the social training that we do. Many of the children we work with are also dealing with various levels of sensory integration issues, and we have found that they have a direct impact on the children's behavior choices. Some of the techniques we have used in sessions and have suggested the children implement in other environments are

- Having an awareness of the children's individual sensory sensitivities
- Taking breaks when the children's attention is waning
- Making sure that there are activities that include motion and gross motor work in each lesson
- Using movement as refocusing and transition activities
- Working with an occupational therapist who is trained in sensory integration

Building our own awareness of the sensory system as it impacts on language skills, processing, and social ability has helped us facilitate children more successfully. We recommend that all adults who are looking to support a child's social development keep sensory awareness as a daily part of their planning. When you see that you are losing a group or an individual child, it is better to give a sensory solution at that time than to push through it or attempt to stop the behavior. As a teacher, sometimes you may find yourself saying, "Come on, let's just get this done." Instead, give everyone a "seventh-inning stretch." The following is a list of cues that children's sensory systems are becoming overwhelmed:

- Tap pens
- Rock in chair
- Squirm on seat
- Talk
- Stare
- Chew on pencil, fingers, gum
- Take longer to answer question
- Tap feet
- Turn around
- Increase negative affect
- Bug and pick on others
- Give disoriented response

When children are having difficulty focusing and staying still, a sensory break is needed. The following are some quick things to suggest that will help children focus during activities.

- Stretch
- Pull up on your chair
- Push down on your desk
- Squeeze your head
- Chew on straw or water bottle
- Squeeze hands
- Push on wall
- Carry something heavy

These activities are also good ideas to use as transitions from one activity to another. Maintain a dialog with occupational therapists about sensory inputs that regulate children. Create lists of things that overwhelm or calm down a particular child. The more opportunities we give children to help them regulate their sensory systems, the more successful they will be.

How to Use This Book

The following is an outline of the book describing each section of the units and how to best implement the activities.

Unit

- All the units are in sequential order.
- You should start at the beginning of the book and work your way through to the end; the units are designed to be completed in order.
- You may choose to skip some of the beginning concepts if you feel your children have mastered them. However, we suggest that the beginning chapters still be introduced to the children so they can learn some of the Wanna Play terms that are used throughout the curriculum.

Social Goals

- The goals are highlighted in each section of the book so it is clear what each one targets. The Social Interactive Checklist can be used to assess the child's present skill level and pick the goal that is appropriate for the child.
- Use these social goals as a guide when developing a child's program and when writing educational plans.

Lesson

- Each lesson will build on the previous lesson.
- Each lesson can also be extracted individually as needed.
- Some children will have a number of these skills already, but they are worth reviewing.

Introduction/Overview

- Purpose
- Introduction to the concept for the adult
- Our opinion on it
- The importance of the skills

- Background information
- Introduction of terms

Teaching Concepts

- The main idea of the lesson
- The skills to be taught
- Belief system the lesson is based on
- The benefit of learning the lesson

Attitude

- Things the adult should remember when going over the lesson
- Suggested attitudes about the concept
- Suggested attitudes about the children
- Attitudes the adults should adopt
- Attitude that should be projected to the student so he or she can take his or her cue from the adult

Lesson Objective

- Observable behaviors for goal tracking
- Intended outcomes of the lesson
- Skills or concepts the child will learn and use

Lesson Introduction

- This section will help the children organize the concepts by giving visual supports that help them retain the concepts.
- Use leading questions to help children develop lists and concept maps. Examples can be found within each lesson introduction.

Concept Mapping

- Draw the bubble maps on a board so the children can have a visual understanding of the layout.
- Example:
  What do we do with our friends? Play
  How do we play? Friendly
  What do you use to play friendly? Use sweet/kind words, use listening, use a safe body, be safe with the toys
- Use pictures to help the children come up with the specific word on the bubble maps.
- If a child gives an answer that is not on the map, use leading question to redirect the child back to the topic being discussed. Do not tell the children that any answer is wrong unless it is a negative concept.

- Feel free to add related answers children think of to the bubble map, even if they are not listed in the curriculum. Try to make sure the words and concepts that are added support the concept map as it is being developed.

Brainstorming and List Making

We use this technique to access what a child already knows about a concept and use it as a springboard to develop new ideas. Like the use of concept mapping, this technique helps the children to tap into their memory and add new information to what they already know.

- Introduce the concept with a clear heading (example: Deciding Who Goes First).
- Use pictures as visual support if needed.
- Have children list as many things as they can that are related to the concept.
- Redirect children when they go off topic by using positive leading questions.
- Use the brainstorming or list-making questions as an assessment tool to find out their concept development on the importance of friendship (example: Who do we look at?).
- Encourage children to think of all the people that they may talk to or interact with during the day. Be sure to include peers and adults in all environments—home, school, social activities, and so forth.
- Help children to think about the times that they need to listen to others for directions or information, look at others when they want something, or want others to listen to them. Use different situations as examples.

Word Defining

- Word defining lesson introductions use similar procedures and strategies as brainstorming and list making.
- Have children share as many definitions of the word as they can think of and list them all.
- When the list is finished, create a definition as a group, similar to the example given in the curriculum.

Activities

- The activities provided in this book are geared toward abilities in children ages 4 to 10. Some of the activities, such as coloring in sweet words, are more appropriate for younger children; activities such as friendship cards are geared toward older children with more expressive abilities such as writing. Consider the ages of the children and their abilities when choosing the activities for your group.

- In the activities section of each lesson, there are games and projects for all types of learners. It is suggested the teacher choose a balance of gross motor, art, game, role-play, writing, group, and individual activities to target all learners in the class.
- There are built-in repetitions of skill learning to utilize repetition as an effective learning tool.
- Use at least three or four activities from each lesson to help children internalize each skill.
- All of the activities listed can also be used separately as fun skill builders throughout the children's day.
- Each activity includes a description of the following:
  Purpose
  Materials
  Preparation
  Procedure

Friendship Cards

Purpose: The friendship cards are used as a visual reminder for the children, to reinforce the concept that has been taught. Many children can internalize the information they learn in a social lesson and even demonstrate the ability to use a skill when discussing an activity or in an artificial role-playing situation. The difficulty occurs in using that skill or strategy in real-time social interaction. The friendship cards are a toolbox of choices that children can draw from and use in the heat of the moment. Use the following materials, preparation, and procedure throughout the curriculum.

Materials: Friendship cards are located in Appendix A. Each card is titled and there is a master list to help keep track of the cards used in each lesson. We suggest using loose-leaf rings or key chains to hold the cards together. We also suggest the cards be glued to index cards for stability.

Preparation: Copy and cut out a set of cards for each child. Glue the cards to index cards and hole punch them to go on the loose-leaf ring or key chain. Choose a location where the cards will be stored that is accessible to the entire class.

Procedure:

1. Give a brief description of what the cards are and how they will be used. Show the children where the cards will be located so that they can find them later. Have children decorate their cover card and put it on their ring. This can be done as part of the first friendship cards lesson.

2. Give each child the card corresponding to the lesson. Have children review the information learned in the lesson and use the visual aids created in the lesson introduction to fill out their cards. Most cards correspond directly with the specific lesson introduction.

3. Have children write or draw to fill in the card. Encourage children to illustrate the card with examples that will help them to remember the information on the card.

4. Have children store cards in an accessible location.

Using Cards in Social Situations

1. When a social situation arises in which a child is having difficulty remembering the social lessons learned, redirect the child to get his or her card.

2. Encourage the child to find the card with the strategy that would help him or her in that specific situation. This step also gives a child a chance to calm down and move away from the scene if he or she is overwhelmed and having difficulty staying calm.

3. Help the child find the strategy that would help him or her in that situation, and then encourage the child to go back to his or her friend and use the tool or social phrase the child chose.

Generalization and Consistency

Not all lessons have or need strategies. However, those that do should be followed to the letter. Some strategies such as the following can be used for multiple lessons.

- Key phrases
- Transitions

In this section of the unit, you will find suggested strategies and techniques that should be integrated into the classroom curriculum and even into the school culture. These strategies are geared toward incidental teaching. They are based on the concept that the moment a child begins struggling with a social situation is the moment he or she should be reminded of the social strategies and techniques the child has been taught.

Social Interaction Checklist

The following Social Interaction Checklist is designed to help identify the social strengths and weaknesses of each child. Have parents and other people in each child's life answer the questions and use the results to choose the goals for each child. Some children will have different goals for different social environments based on social and sensory experiences. These goals have been laid out in a progression, and we suggest working through them in order from Eye Contact and Interaction to Social Awareness.

Name: _____

Start Date: _____

Eye Contact and Interaction	Always	Sometimes	Not Yet
Child will make eye contact with peers and adults when they are requesting interaction from the child.			
Child will make eye contact when listening to directions.			
Child will make eye contact when name is called.			
Child will use eye contact and facial expressions together.			
Child will use eye contact as a cue when attempting to engage others in interaction.			
Child will maintain conversational eye contact for the entire verbal interaction with peer or adult.			

(Continued)

(Continued)

	Always	Sometimes	Not yet
Child will maintain eye contact and hold interest with a speaker in a group discussion or classroom setting for the length of the presentation.			
Child will retain information from a speaker in a group discussion or classroom setting for the length of the presentation.			
Child will choose activities that include others over solitary activities.			
Child will engage in reciprocal activities with another child.			
Child will engage in reciprocal activities with an adult.			
Child will join activities with others when invited.			
Child will choose (unprompted/unfacilitated) to complete a game with another child.			
Child will choose (unprompted/unfacilitated) to complete a game with a group.			
Child will choose (unprompted/unfacilitated) to complete a multistep task.			
Communication	*Always*	*Sometimes*	*Not yet*
Child will use a system to clearly communicate wants, needs, and ideas to others.			
Child will use sweet words and phrases when requesting something from peers and adults.			
Child will use a kind, polite tone of voice when communicating with others.			
Child will restate him- or herself when not understood and ask others to repeat themselves when he or she does not understand.			
Child will stay on topic when contributing to a group discussion in a classroom setting.			
Child will use prompted phrases to initiate with others in a group setting.			
Child will use prompts to make suggestions to peers during group activities.			
Child will make positive suggestions to peers of original ideas during group activities.			

Appropriate Body Behavior	Always	Sometimes	Not yet
Child will choose a positive, proactive affect in all social situations.			
Child will use visual, verbal, and physical techniques to calm him- or herself in a conflict situation.			
Child will use positive interactions and behaviors to get attention.			
Child will use sensory input to gain and maintain control of emotional level.			
Child will respect personal space of peers and adults.			
Child will use sensory suggestions when prompted by an adult.			
Child will use sensory suggestions when needed without prompting.			
Child will use appropriate levels of movement and energy for different activities and environments.			
Child will have an appropriate response to different situations.			
Play	Always	Sometimes	Not yet
Child will allow expansion of repetitious play by a peer or adult.			
Child will wander about and does not become involved in any activity. (Unoccupied play*)			
Child will play alone, with no awareness of or involvement with other children. (Solitary play*)			
Child will watch others play without entering the activities. (Onlooker play*)			
Child will play with similar objects clearly beside other children with slight acknowledgement of the others. (Parallel play*)			
Child will engage in unstructured interactive play with similar toys with other children. (Associative play*)			
Child will engage in structured group play with rules and goals. (Cooperative play*)			
Child will invite a peer to play with him or her.			

(Continued)

(Continued)

	Always	Sometimes	Not yet
Child will join another child or group of children if asked in play, game, or activity.			
Child will ask to join another child or group of children in play, game, or activity.			
Child will attempt to join another child or group of children in play by making a suggestion to add onto the game or activity.			
Child will follow a play theme until game or activity is finished.			
Child will use/show good sportsmanship in a game by cheering on a peer.			
Social Awareness	*Always*	*Sometimes*	*Not yet*
Child will identify his or her own strengths and needs and that of his or her peers.			
Child will use encouraging phrases and actions in games and activities with peers.			
Child will verbally show appreciation for other by using "please," "thank you," and apologies.			
Child will physically show appreciation for others by including others and sharing.			
Child will use skills, organize others, give directions, listen to ideas, and encourage participation to lead a group.			
Child will stay on topic when contributing to a group discussion in a classroom setting.			
Child will respect personal space of peers and adults during a group activity.			
Child will use the skills taught to maintain focus and attention in a group environment.			
Child will learn about the various roles in a group and skills necessary to successfully work in each role.			
Child will learn to ask for help when needed when he or she is not able to listen or attend.			
Child will increase his or her ability to participate in a group by learning how to listen.			
Child will learn how to listen to others' ideas and show respect for them, even if the child may not agree.			

NOTE: *Parten, M. B. (1932). Social participation among preschool children. *Journal of Abnormal Psychology, 27,* 243–269.

Discovering Friendship

The skills needed to make positive friendships should be taught to all children and are skills that will help them interact in relationships throughout their lives. Often, defining and discussing who friends are and the importance of friendship will help to increase children's appreciation of their friends. The children will then make attempts to strive for better friendships with the friends they already have. Teaching the skills in this unit will build children's understanding of why the skills in the units that follow are important to learn. Building better relationships and having friends is the reason we need to learn to use kind words, look at our friends, listen to our friends, and learn how to play games and how to work in a group.

Social Goals

- Children will greet peers and adults as well as respond to greetings and salutations without prompting.
- Children will restate themselves when not understood and ask others to repeat themselves when they do not understand.
- Children will physically show appreciation of others by including others and sharing.
- Children will invite a peer to play with them.
- Children will use a system to clearly communicate their wants, needs, and ideas to others.

LESSON 1: WHAT IS A FRIEND?

Introduction/Overview

The Lesson Introduction for this unit begins by asking children to define both a friend and friendship. This allows the children to think more specifically about what a friend means and what they need to do to build friendships with others. Begin using the term friend whenever you are referring to others in the group. Children may not necessarily consider each child a friend, but they will benefit from using positive friendship skills whenever they interact with others.

Teaching Concepts

- We need to include others in what we do in order to build friendships.
- Things are more fun to do when we are with our friends.
- A friendship can begin with the first hello.

Attitude

- Observing the children and complimenting their attempts at using positive friendship skills is the best way to reinforce the concepts we want them to learn.
- Even the children that prefer to be by themselves will benefit from learning these concepts when they have to interact with others.
- Support the children with positive verbal reinforcement if they need to be encouraged to include others and think of them as friends.

Lesson Objective

- Children will learn what they need to say and do to make friends with others.
- Children will think about how to include others in their games and activities.
- Children will learn phrases and actions that make being a friend fun.

Lesson Introduction

Brainstorm for Key Concepts

Have children develop lists to refer to by asking specific questions. Use the directions found in the "How to Use This Book" section. Here are some suggestions for questions to ask:

- What is friendship?
- Who are your friends?

- What are fun things to do with friends?
- Why are friends great?

Activities

Friendship Collage

Purpose: This activity will expand on the ideas children have about things they can do with their friends. Children will often only choose one or two things to play. Using pictures can help them think of fun new things to play.

Materials: Old toy catalogs and children's magazines; scissors; glue sticks; large piece or 8 ½ × 11 pieces of white paper, or letters cut out of construction paper to spell "friendship."

Preparation: Gather supplies.

Procedure:

1. Explain that the children are to look through the catalogs or magazines for pictures of toys, games, or children playing together.

2. Have them cut out the pictures they find. Help with the cutting if necessary.

3. The pictures can then be glued on individual sheets or on one large sheet of paper as a group.

4. You can have them glue the pictures onto the friendship letters first, then glue the letters on the poster.

5. Write a heading on the poster, such as "Things We Do With Friends."

Friendship Acrostic Poem

Purpose: Brainstorming friendship words will begin to help the children think of all the ways to be a good friend. This activity can either be done as a group or individually.

Materials: Large paper for poster, construction paper, or white 8 ½ × 11 paper

Preparation: Cut the letters to the word "friendship" out of construction paper and glue them vertically down the left edge of a poster-size piece of paper, or write the word friendship vertically down an 8 ½ × 11 piece of paper for each child.

Procedure:

1. Have children brainstorm as a group or individually think of friendship words that begin with each letter of the word friendship.

Using books about friendship can also help them be more creative in the words they choose.

2. Use the lists that were made in the lesson introduction as reminders of friendship words.

3. Write the words next to the letter using the letter to begin the word.

4. Hang the poster or individual poems in the room as reminders of friendship.

Friends 2-by-2 Game

Purpose: This is a great game for the children to begin interacting with other children, find out something about a friend, and become more comfortable with pretending.

Materials: Even number of 3 × 5 cards, enough for each child in the class to have one

Preparation: Make pairs of cards with the same animal on them (one pair of cards for each animal). If reading is still challenging, write the words and have a picture of the animal. Example: 2 lion cards, 2 bear cards, 2 dog cards, etc.

Procedure:

1. Have each child pick a card.

2. Make sure all the cards are used so each child is matched with another child. If there is an odd number of students, have an adult participate in the game.

3. Explain that they must act out the animal on their card and find a friend who is being the same animal that they are. They cannot ask their friends; they have to figure it out by what the other children are doing.

4. Once they find their "twin" animal, then they can talk. They must find out one thing about the other child. You may need to help by giving them a category or question. Examples: "What is your favorite TV show?" "What is your favorite game?"

5. When they have finished finding out the answer to the questions, have the children share what they found out about their friend with the group.

Friendship Cards—Discovering Friendships

Purpose: The friendship cards are used as a visual reminder for the children, to reinforce the concept that has been taught.

Materials: The following friendship cards found in Appendix A

- Friendship
- Why Friends Are Great

Preparation: See directions in "How to Use This Book."

Procedure: See directions in "How to Use This Book."

Generalization and Consistency

- Use the term "friend" whenever you are referring to the children interacting with their peers. This will encourage the thought that it is good to make friendships and friends are fun.
- Verbally acknowledge all positive interactions and point out all use of friendship skills when children are interacting.
- Make all activities opportunities to build friendships.

LESSON 2: MAKING NEW FRIENDS

Introduction/Overview

The way we interact with new friends can be very different from how we interact with friends we have known for awhile. This lesson will help the children to initiate interactions and friendships and learn how to differentiate these relationships from friendships that they have already made with others.

Teaching Concepts

- The use of greetings to initiate interactions with others.
- The things we need to say to make friends.
- The things we need to do to make friends.

Attitude

- Friendship skills need to be taught and modeled.
- Just because the children may not know the things to do or say to be a friend does not mean they do not want to make friends.
- Even though some children may play alone, they will benefit from learning how to make friends.

Lesson Objectives

- Children will learn different ways to make friends.
- Children will learn different places to look for friends and ways to tell if others want to be their friends.
- Learning things about others is a way to make friends.

Lesson Introduction

Brainstorm for Key Concepts

Have children develop lists to refer to by asking them specific questions. Use the directions found in the "How to Use This Book" section. Here are some suggestions of questions to ask:

- What are ways to say hello?
- What are ways to say good-bye?
- What are the words to say to introduce yourself?

Activities

Meatball

Purpose: In this activity, children spend time asking questions about the people in the group. It will help them find out more about the other kids in their group.

Materials: Small ball, polyspots, or sit-upons to designate the spot where the child needs to sit (if needed)

Preparation: Set up spots in circle for children to sit on.

Procedure:

1. With all children sitting in circle, have them take turns passing the ball to one another.

2. Have children say the name of the person they are passing to and ask the person a question about him- or herself.

3. Give suggestions of what to ask about if the children are having trouble thinking of what to say. Examples: What is your favorite food? (or favorite TV show, favorite color, etc.)

Friend, Friend, What Do You See?

Purpose: This activity is based on the book, *Brown Bear, Brown Bear, What Do You See?* by Eric Carle. Do the activity as explained and then adapt it to allow the children to look at their friends and notice things about them.

Materials: The book *Brown Bear, Brown Bear, What Do You See?* by Eric Carle, Puppets for Brown Bear Template found in Appendix B, sticks for the puppets, crayons or markers, scissors, and tape

Preparation: Make copies of the puppets, enough for each child to color at least one.

Procedure:

1. Read the "Brown Bear" book.

2. Have each child color and cut out at least one puppet. Make sure you have at least one puppet of every animal in the story.

3. Tape each puppet to a stick.

4. Reread the story. Every time a new animal is mentioned, have the children with that animal raise their puppets. The children are usually very familiar with the story and enjoy saying the story while you read.

5. Then have the children take turns saying, "Friend, friend, what do you see?" looking at one of the children in the group.

6. The child they are looking at must then say one thing he or she sees when looking at the other child. Example: "I see a happy smile looking at me," or "I see blonde hair looking at me."

7. If the children have started to learn things about each other, encourage them to say the things they know about the other child. Example: "I see a kid who loves cars looking at me."

Introduce Yourself

Purpose: Using the words we know to say hello and let people know we want to be friends. Learn that we say hello differently to different people in different places.

Materials: People Flashcards and Place Flashcards found in Appendix B

Preparation: Cut out cards found in Appendix A. Draw pictures on cards or help the children to read the cards when it is their turn.

Procedure:

1. Divide the cards into two piles, one of people cards and one of places cards.

2. Have each child take a turn and pick a card from the people pile and the place pile.

3. Role-play saying "hello," pretending another child is that person.

4. Discuss the difference places and appropriate interactions for each place.

Making Friends Handout

Purpose: This activity is suited for use in a group or one-on-one session. The statements or questions listed will begin the child's thinking of who he or she might want to attempt being friends with and what to say when he or she decides to try to make a friend.

Materials: "Making Friends" handout found in Appendix B

Preparation: Make copies of handout for each child.

Procedure:

1. Give each child a handout.

2. Explain the questions or statements. Give suggestions for possible responses.

3. Also explain that the person they think of may be someone they have talked to before or someone that they just think it might be fun to be friends with.

4. Have them draw a picture of themselves and that person on the last page doing something fun together.

Lifestories Game by FNDI Limited Partnership

Purpose: This is a great game to find out more about other people. It asks different questions and encourages the players to tell different stories and things about themselves and their family. Basic reading skills are helpful. If there are some stronger readers in the group, encourage the children to ask each other for help reading if they need it.

Materials: Lifestories game

Preparation: Read the directions to be able to explain them to the children. You might also let the children learn how to play on their own as a group activity.

Procedure: Follow the directions included in the game.

Friendship Cards—Discovering Friendships

Purpose: The friendship cards are used as a visual reminder for the children, to reinforce the concept that has been taught.

Materials: The following friendship cards found in Appendix A:

- Ways to Say Hello
- Ways to Introduce Yourself

Preparation: See directions in "How to Use This Book."

Procedure: See directions in "How to Use This Book."

Generalization and Consistency

- Acknowledge any attempts by the children to interact with someone new.
- Provide opportunities for the children to get another child's attention by calling his or her name. This will help the children to learn the names of the others.

- Remember interesting facts about the children and use them during conversations so they will see how great it is to know things about people as they are making friends.

LESSON 3: BUILDING FRIENDSHIPS

Introduction/Overview

Teaching the skills to build friendships is as important as teaching how to make friends. It takes effort to keep friendships going and to try to make deeper relationships with others. This lesson will take the skills learned in the first lesson and expand on them to build friendships with peers.

Teaching Concepts

- Making friends is fun.
- Making friends takes effort.
- Thinking about our friends helps to make friendships.
- Finding out about our friends is part of making friends.

Attitude

- Making the extra effort to be a friend needs our positive guidance and support.
- Friendship skills need to be taught step by step.
- Help children to learn the importance of friends by talking about the friendships in their lives and your own.
- Acknowledge children when they are using positive friendship skills with others.

Lesson Objective

- Children will learn the step-by-step skills needed to make friendships.
- Children will learn the benefit of making the extra effort to build friendships.
- Children will learn questions to ask to build friendships.

Lesson Introduction

Concept Map—"What Do You Need to Do to Build Friendships?"

Have the children help develop a concept map by asking leading questions. Use the directions found in the "How to Use This Book" section.

Figure 1.1 What Do We Need to Do to Build Friendships?

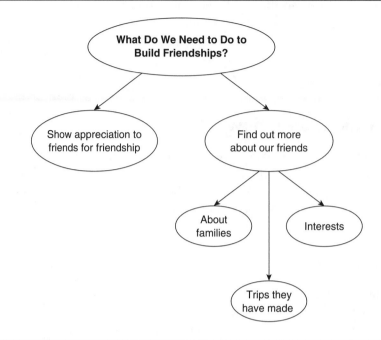

Activities

Friend Bingo

Purpose: This activity will help children learn questions to ask to make friends and find out more things about their friends.

Materials: "Friend Bingo" worksheet found in Appendix B, markers or crayons

Preparation: Add pictures to the bingo sheet to help the children who are not reading yet.

Procedure:

1. Give each child a worksheet and a marker or crayon.

2. Have all the children walk around and ask the other children who has things on the sheet or who has done the things on the sheet.

3. You can either have them ask until they have four in a row or fill out the whole sheet before yelling "BINGO."

Gift of Friendship

Purpose: To have children think of special things they can do for or say to friends to show their appreciation for the friendship. This activity can focus on building friendships within the group and also help the children to think of other friendships in their lives.

Materials: The "Gift of Friendship" handout found in Appendix B, marker or crayons

Preparation: Make copies of the handout for each child.

Procedure:

1. Discuss or make a list of different things to say or things to do to say thank you to a friend for being a friend.

2. Encourage children to use words of appreciation as gifts instead of toys.

3. Have the children think of a friend they want to give a gift to and decorate the gift with the words and any additional decoration they want to add.

4. You can use this activity again at holidays or for birthday celebrations.

Charades for Kids by Pressman Toy Co.

Purpose: This is a great game to help young children build confidence about interacting with friends so they can make friendships grow.

Materials: Charades for Kids board game

Preparation: Read the directions to be able to explain them to the children.

Procedure: Play the game using the instructions included with the game.

Write a Letter to a Friend

Purpose: This activity gives children a chance to reflect on what they appreciate about the friends they have just made. It can be used after the children have been together for a short while or at the end of a whole school year.

Materials: Copies of the handout "Letter to a Friend" found in Appendix B

Preparation: Make copies of handout for each child.

Procedure:

1. Explain the purpose of the letter and that this is a time to thank the friend or friends for the opportunity of meeting them and becoming friends.

2. If working with a group of children, encourage them to choose someone from that group.

3. Collect all the letters at the end and hand them out later or put them in backpacks to be taken home.

4. Explain that they are to keep who they wrote to or how many letters they got to themselves. This helps to minimize the possibility of hurt feelings on the part of the children that didn't receive as many letters.

5. Note the children who did not receive any letters and use it as an opportunity to teach more friendship skills.

Friendship Cards—Discovering Friendships

Purpose: The friendship cards are used as a visual reminder for the children to reinforce the concept that has been taught.

Materials: The following friendship cards found in Appendix A:

- Ways to Show Appreciation
- Things We Can Find Out About Friends

Preparation: See directions in "How to Use This Book."

Procedure: See directions in "How to Use This Book."

Generalization and Consistency

- Finding out information about the people we want to be friends with is a great way to make friends. Prompt the children with questions to ask others so they can find out more about them.
- Working in pairs encourages friendships and helps children find out more about the other children.
- Use the common interests of the children as ways of linking them to each other. For example, group by "dinosaur lovers" for an activity.

LESSON 4: RELATIONSHIPS WITH DIFFERENT TYPES OF FRIENDS

Introduction/Overview

Children have the opportunity to meet friends in different places and to make different types of friends. Some people are easier to be friends with than others, and we also have different types of relationships with different friends. Having different types of friends and different types of relationships requires us to think about what things we want to do or say with what friends.

Teaching Concepts

- Thinking about the different types of people in the children's world and how relationships may be different.

- The qualities to look for in friends.
- The qualities we want to have to be a good friend.
- Treating others with kindness as the best way to be a friend.

Attitude

- Some of the children may not understand that they need to think about appropriate interactions depending on who they are interacting with and where they are.
- Everyone has positive qualities.
- Everyone can learn to be more positive when they are making friends.

Lesson Objectives

- Children will learn about different types of friends.
- Children will discover positive qualities in themselves.
- Children will learn what positive qualities to look for in others to build friendships.

Lesson Introduction

Concept Map—"Types of Friends"

Have the children help develop a concept map by asking leading questions. Use the directions found in the "How to Use This Book" section.

Figure 1.2   Types of Friends

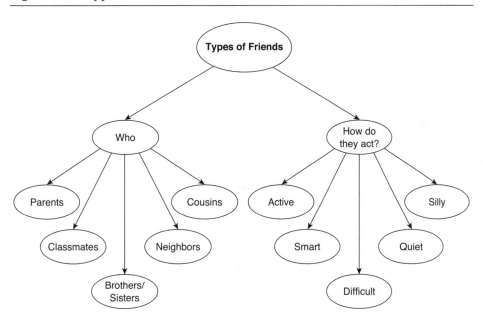

Activities

School Friends and Best Friends Cartoons

Purpose: To help children think of new and different things to say and do with friends. This will also help them to differentiate how well they know various people and what it means to be a best friend.

Materials: "Types of Friends" handout found in Appendix B, markers or crayons

Preparation: Make copies of handout for each child.

Procedure:

1. Either brainstorm lists or talk about the things we do with our friends at school and the things we do with our best friends.

2. Refer back to the concept map in the lesson introduction to talk about different types of friends and how they act.

3. Have children think of something they would do with each type of friend and what they would be saying.

4. Have them color a cartoon for each.

5. Older children may want to color several cartoon boxes to make a comic strip.

Friendship Quilt

Purpose: This activity will introduce the concept of positive qualities. You may need to define positive qualities for the children. You can also substitute "good things we like about others" or "great ways to be a friend" to help children think about the wonderful positive friendship qualities they have and their friends have.

Materials: "Friendship Quilt" pages found in Appendix B, markers, large paper

Preparation: Make copies of the quilt squares for each child.

Procedure:

1. Brainstorm the great things about the children and their friends. Ask children why they like to be friends with them. Also point out the qualities that make the children good friends to others.

2. Have the children choose a quality and write it on the square. Then have them draw a picture of themselves and their friend showing the quality they have picked.

3. Write "Friendship Quilt" on a large paper and hang it on the wall.

4. When the children finish their quilt square, have them glue it to the quilt on the wall.

5. Have the children make several squares to fill the quilt.

Group It

Purpose: This activity will encourage children to interact more with the others in the group and help teach the idea that the more we learn about our friends, the more fun we will have with them.

Materials: Packet of index cards

Preparation: Write a different category on each card. Choose a variety of categories about which the children will be able to easily think of an idea. If reading is still challenging, use pictures along with the words.

Procedure:

1. Have each child pick a card and read or tell what it says.

2. Explain that the children must then walk around and find the other children that like the same thing that they do from that category.

3. If food is the category, then explain that they must all think of their favorite food and find others who like the same thing.

Friendship Cards—Discovering Friendships

Purpose: The friendship cards are used as a visual reminder for the children, to reinforce the concept that has been taught.

Materials: The following friendship cards found in Appendix A:

- How Our Friends Act
- Our Friends

Preparation: See directions in "How to Use This Book."

Procedure: See directions in "How to Use This Book."

Generalization and Consistency

- Acknowledge any and all attempts children make to show appreciation to a friend.
- When a child does something for another child or for you, show your appreciation for this effort by saying, "Thank you. You are such a good friend to do (whatever he or she did) or say (whatever he or she said)."

- Encourage children to ask questions when interacting with another child. Prompt the idea or the exact words if necessary.
- When children begin to make a friendship, acknowledge it by telling them what they have done to try to be a friend.

Making Eye Contact for Interaction

"The eyes are the windows to the soul," the proverb says, which is why they deserve a unit of their own. This is the beginning of all interactions. Eye contact with infants is the key form of communication. It is how they learn about the world around them. Children use eye contact to develop their perception of trust and what is a constant in the world. Through the years of development, children use eye contact to explore and learn. It is key in learning the forms of communication such as language, gesture, and expression. Without eye contact, it would be much harder to get information about the world around us.

The key to success in this program is an emphasis on developing eye contact frequency and duration. There are many factors that come into play when children are not making eye contact. Some of these include visual sensitivity, auditory sensitivity, sensory overstimulation, or even a lack of understanding of the role of eye contact in interaction. We need to remember, as those responsible for the social development of a child, that if the child is not making eye contact, he or she is not engaging, attending, or focusing.

Children are tricky when it comes to avoiding eye contact. They are more vested in avoidance than we are. This avoidance is a safety mechanism for them, and therefore they will try to hold onto it as much as they can.

Social Goals

- Children will understand the importance of eye contact as an interactive tool.
- Children will make eye contact when listening to adults and peers.

- Children will make eye contact when making a request of an adult or child.
- Children will make eye contact when telling stories and relaying experiences to adults and other children.

LESSON 1: WHAT IS EYE CONTACT?

Introduction/Overview

In this lesson, we will explore the meaning and importance of eye contact. We want teachers to use this time to assess the children's understanding of what it means to make eye contact or look at others.

Teaching Concepts

- Eye contact is looking into someone's eyes in a way that has meaning.
- Eye contact is helpful and important.
- Eye contact is an important component of communication and is needed to increase attention and focus.
- Eye contact needs to be practiced in controlled situations to make it easier in natural environments.
- Sometimes we need to work on making eye contact to get better at it.
- Eye contact is held as much as possible for the whole of the interaction.

Attitude

Although eye contact is challenging and children will resist it, we still need to teach it with a positive attitude.

This concept needs to be worked on until the children are able to use eye contact effectively.

- We can't assume children will have a conscious awareness of what eye contact is.
- Making and holding eye contact is not always easy, and the skill is often taken for granted.
- Not making eye contact is not always a sign of insolence, guilt, or ignoring the other person.

Lesson Objective

- Children will identify looking at one's eyes as eye contact.
- Children will identify who to look at when interacting.
- Children will have experience with making eye contact for a long duration.

Lesson Introduction

Brainstorm for Key Concepts

Have children develop lists to refer to by asking them specific questions. Use the directions found in the "How to Use This Book" section. Here are some suggestions for questions to ask:

- Who do we look at?
- Why do we look at other people?
- Why do other people look at us?

Activities

Staring Contest

Purpose: This activity enables the children to have the physical experience of making and holding eye contact.

Materials: None

Preparation: None

Procedure:

1. Have children pair off.

2. Explain to the children that they need to look into their friend's eyes until you say stop.

3. Children are allowed to blink, but not to talk (they will ask).

4. Start with 15 seconds for the first contest.

5. Ask children how long they think the contest lasted and let them know the time so they can get some idea of how the time seems longer when we are making direct eye contact.

6. Do the activity a few more times, gradually increasing the duration.

7. Make it fun!

Silly Glasses

Purpose: Many children need a little visual interest to help them to attend. Visual distracters in their environment make it difficult for them to cue in and stay present with someone. This activity is a fun, silly way to help.

Materials: "Silly Glasses" template found in Appendix B, cardboard, glue, stickers, and craft decorations

Preparation: Cut out a pair of glasses for each child in your class (see template).

Procedure:

1. Remind children of the importance of looking at one another in the eyes.

2. Tell the children that they are going to make something to help them remember how important eye contact is.

3. Have children use craft decorations, stickers, and markers to embellish the glasses.

4. Teacher makes a pair for him- or herself.

5. If the majority of the class is challenged on eye contact, the teacher should wear glasses when giving important instructions. Phase out the visual cue by gradually not using the glasses, but pretending to put them on to help the children remember.

Eye Contact Tag

Purpose: This gross motor game is beneficial for the kinesthetic learner. The physical movement and body language of the activity helps these learners internalize the act of making eye contact.

Materials: Polyspots, sit-upons, or other mats for children to stand on

Preparation: None

Procedure:

1. One child is "it."

2. All other children are on a spot.

3. The child who is "it" goes around the room, trying to get the other children to look into his or her eyes.

4. The child who is "it" cannot touch or get too close to others. Remind children that this is a game where sweet words are to be used.

5. If the child who is "it" gets someone to look at him or her, that person is then "it" as well, and must go and get as many others as possible.

6. Play until there is only one "not-it" child remaining. Then start the game over with that child being "it."

7. When working with large groups of younger children, hoops can be used instead of spots to support the use of appropriate body space.

Friendship Cards—Using Eye Contact

Purpose: The friendship cards are used as a visual reminder for the children, to reinforce the concept that has been taught.

Materials: The following friendship cards found in Appendix A:

- Why We Look at Other People
- Why Other People Look at Us

Preparation: See directions in "How to Use This Book."

Procedure: See directions in "How to Use This Book."

Generalization and Consistency

- Use praise and behavior-specific feedback every time the children make appropriate eye contact to help them to identify what eye contact actually is.

LESSON 2: LOOKING TO TALK

Introduction/Overview

Many of the children we work with who have poor eye contact also have difficulty initiating interactions with other children. Sometimes they can have the same difficulty with adults. What we have found is that these children are not using eye contact as a verbal cue in communication.

Teaching Concepts

- Looking tells people that we are talking to them.
- Looking tells people how we feel about what we are saying.
- Looking tells people when we are done talking and that it's their turn to talk.

Attitude

- It is our own responsibility to make sure we are heard and other people are listening.
- If children are not making eye contact with a person, then they are not talking to that person.

Lesson Objectives

- Children will make eye contact when requesting something from an adult or peer.
- Children will make eye contact when they are telling stories and sharing information with adults and peers.

Lesson Introduction

Concept Map—"Looking to Talk"

Have children develop a concept map to refer to by asking leading questions. Use the directions found in the "How to Use This Book" section.

Figure 2.1   Looking to Talk Concept Map

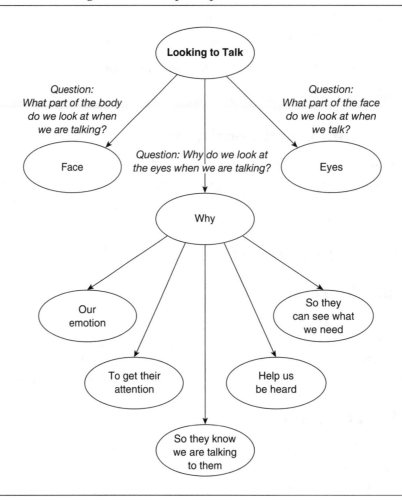

Suggested Questions

- What part of the other person's body do we look at when we are talking? (face)
- What part of the face do we look at? (eyes)
- Why do we look at the eyes when we are talking? (to see their emotions and show our own, to get their attention, so they know we are talking to them, helps us to be heard, so they can see what we need)

Activities

"Why We Look" Poster

Purpose: Many children learn from lists and visual references that may be hung in the classroom. This is a fun way to create something that is meaningful and visually interesting that can be referenced for the rest of the school year.

Materials: Poster paper, "Eye Coloring Sheet" found in Appendix B.

Preparation: On poster paper, recreate the list of why we look at others when we talk to them. Make copy of "Eyes Coloring Sheet" for each child in class.

Procedure:

Review the list of why we look when we talk.

Have children color in their eyes and cut them out to add to poster.

Zoom and Schwartz

Purpose: This game is a great way to help children work on attending to who is making eye contact with them. It also helps the sequencing skills needed for following a group discussion.

Materials: None

Preparation: None

Procedure:

1. The object of the game is to keep the conversation going as long as possible.

2. The conversation has only two words, "Zoom" and "Schwartz."

3. Sit children in a circle.

4. The first child says "Zoom" to someone, and then that child says "Schwartz" to the next child. The children need to use eye contact to indicate who should go next.

5. If a child misses his or her cue because he or she is not looking, or says one of the words but does not use eye contact, then that child is out.

Talking Down the Lane

Purpose: This is another opportunity for children to practice saying things to others' eyes.

Materials: None

Preparation: None

Procedure:

1. Someone picks a funny phrase for the whole group to use.

2. Each child takes a turn saying the funny phrase to another child in the group.

3. Each child needs to pay attention to the eye contact the other children are making with others in the class so that he or she knows when it is his or her turn.

4. If a child misses his or her cue because he or she is not looking, or says one of the words without using eye contact, then that child is out.

5. When a child is out, he or she must think of the next silly phrase.

Name Ball

Purpose: This game works on the same concepts as Zoom and Schwartz and Talking Down the Lane, but it adds a physical item that will help children track who is addressing who.

Materials: Tennis ball or small rubber ball

Preparation: None

Procedure:

1. Have children sit in a circle.

2. The object of the game is to cue the person you are going to throw the ball to by making direct, sustained eye contact with him or her.

3. Explain that the person throwing the ball must be sure that the person he or she wants to throw to is looking directly at him or her.

4. Either have the group work as a team with the goal of playing for 2 minutes with the lowest number of drops; or play so that if the ball drops, the person who threw the ball is out. This will cause the children to take more care in ensuring the person catching is looking and attending.

5. After the first round, challenge the children to do it again with fewer drops.

What Do I Mean?—Charades

Purpose: To begin or expand the children's understanding of the importance of looking at someone to be able to recognize the person's emotions when interacting with him or her.

Materials: Emotion Flashcards and Social Phrases Flashcards found in Appendix B

Preparation: Use two sets of cards, one with emotions and the other with phrases.

Procedure:

1. Put the group in pairs or choose a volunteer to be the first to participate.

2. Have one of the children pick a card from each set.

3. Ask that child to read the phrase aloud and use the appropriate emotion in his or her voice and face.

4. Have the other child, or remainder of the group, guess the emotion.

5. To expand on the activity, have the child first read the phrase aloud facing away from the other child or group. If children are not able to guess the emotion, have the child face the others and read the phrase again.

Friendship Cards—Using Eye Contact

Purpose: The friendship cards are used as a visual reminder for the children, to reinforce the concept that has been taught.

Materials: The following friendship cards found in Appendix A:

- Where We Look When We Are Talking
- Why We Look at the Eyes When We Are Talking

Preparation: See directions in "How to Use This Book."

Procedure: See directions in "How to Use This Book."

Generalization and Consistency

To encourage eye contact, try the following:

- Request eye contact from the children at every opportunity. Use visual prompts such as pointing to your eyes, holding objects of interest up to the face, or making silly faces.
- Use the list of why we look at people to give behavior-specific feedback to children on their eye contact when talking.
- Ask for eye contact when the children are making statements or requesting objects.
- If children ask questions or request something without eye contact, either do not respond until they look at you, or tell them you cannot hear what they are saying unless they are looking at you: "Are you asking/talking to me or are you asking/talking to (what the children are looking at)?"

LESSON 3: LOOKING TO LISTEN

Introduction/Overview

All children with attention issues will improve their ability to focus if their eye contact is strengthened and supported in the classroom. If the children are not visually attending, it is too easy for their minds to wander and to get fragmented and disjointed information. Focused eye contact can also aid those with auditory processing issues. On the other side of the interaction, the speaker will have difficulty determining if the child is still listening. Adults can react by assuming the child is being defiant or unfocused, and other children can think the child is uninterested in playing.

Teaching Concepts

- Looking is listening.
- We need to be looking at those with whom we are speaking so they know we are listening. If we look away, the speaker will think we are not listening.
- We try to look at people for the entire time they are talking so we hear every word they say.
- We need to do three things to listen: look (make eye contact), hear (understand), and think (remember).

Attitude

- What the children want to say is interesting.
- This is a skill to be learned, not an action to be forced, therefore avoid physical prompting.
- Eye contact is the key to listening and showing that we are listening to others.
- Listening is very difficult in visually and auditorily challenging situations.
- Visual and tactical supports should be used to help with listening.

Lesson Objectives

- Children will hold eye contact with their peers and adults when receiving directions.
- Children will hold eye contact with their peers and adults for stories and discussion.
- Children will track from speaker to speaker in group discussion.
- Children will make sustained eye contact when listening to an adult.
- Children will make sustained eye contact when listening to other children.
- Children's attention and eye contact will move from one speaker to another.
- Children will follow multistep directions for a game.
- Children will list reasons why listening is important in relationships.
- Children will use responsive facial expressions to show they are listening.

Lesson Introduction

Concept Map—"Looking to Listen"

Have children develop a concept map to refer to by asking leading questions. Use the directions found in the "How to Use This Book" section.

Figure 2.2   Looking to Listen Concept Map

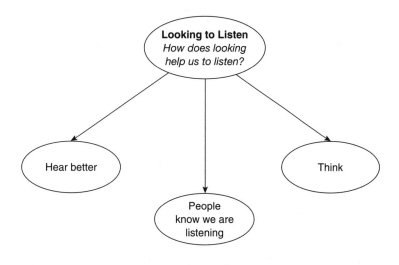

Activities

Mirror Game

Purpose: This game is perfect for developing the duration of interactive eye contact. The success lies in its silliness. Also, the participants will encourage each other to hold eye contact.

Materials: None

Preparation: None

Procedure:

1. Pair off the children and have them sit facing their partner.

2. In each pair, one child is the actor and the other is the mirror.

3. The actor moves his or her arms and makes different facial expressions.

4. The mirror must follow the actor exactly.

5. Remind actors that they can cue their mirror if he or she stops attending.

6. After a minute, have the actor and mirror switch roles. Keep switching back and forth, increasing the amount of time the children stay in a role.

Silent Simon Says

Purpose: This activity is key for children who have poor eye contact, but have not been challenged on it because they will attend enough to pick up most of the verbal directions. This activity will illustrate for the child how much can be missed when we are not looking to learn.

Materials: None

Preparation: None

Procedure:

1. Each person takes a turn being Simon—the one who initiates the action that the others must follow.

2. Simon is not allowed to talk.

3. Simon makes a gesture or facial expressions that the other children must imitate.

4. If someone misses a motion, he or she sits down.

5. For younger children, give a small verbal cue like "try/do this."

6. For older children, do action quickly and then put hands down. Let the children know they need to hold the motion.

7. For an extra challenge, have Simon do two activities at the same time, such as touch nose/stick out tongue.

Storytelling Game

Purpose: This game will help the children to see how much easier it is to hear and understand what people are saying when they are making eye contact.

Materials: None

Preparation: None

Procedure:

1 Have the class split into teams. For smaller groups, have children compete individually.

2. Facilitator tells a story with three specific details.

3. Team members raise their hand and tell what they remember. Give each team a point for what they remember.

4. Use visual cues, such as memory cards, that will help the children remember what the story was about (e.g., use a picture of a pair of sneakers and tell a story about your favorite sneakers).

5. To expand the activity, divide children into pairs. Have them take turns telling a story after which their partners tell what they remember.

Guess a Doodle

Purpose: Children need to make eye contact to attend to the clues in order to guess the answer.

Materials: Guess a Doodle by Pressman Toy Co., or picture cards found in Appendix B.

Preparation: Cut quarter-page pieces of scrap paper so each child has 5 to 10 of them.

Procedure:

1. Someone is the describer, and the rest of the children are the artists.

2. The person describing picks a card and gives clues for the others to guess what is on the card.

3. The others do not call out loud, but rather draw a picture of what they think is on the card.

4. After all clues are given, all the children share their pictures to see who was right.

Friendship Cards—Using Eye Contact

Purpose: The friendship cards are used as a visual reminder for the children, to reinforce the concept that has been taught.

Materials: The following friendship card found in Appendix A: How Looking Helps Us to Listen

Preparation: See directions in "How to Use This Book."

Procedure: See directions in "How to Use This Book."

Generalization and Consistency

- Minimize the visual and auditory distractions when requesting the child's listening and attention. This will allow the children to focus on and process what is being said. (Sidebar conversation and other adults talking on the side will challenge the children's ability to hear, let alone listen.)
- Ask for eye contact when the children are making statements or requesting objects.
- Use gestures, such as pointing to nose while talking, to cue the children about using eye contact when listening.
- When answering a child's question, stop speaking the moment the child looks away and do not start speaking again until his or her eye contact comes back.
- If you lose the children's eye contact during directions, stop talking until the children's eye contact comes back to you.
- Help children lengthen the duration of listening by giving directions or answering questions slowly so they need to hold eye contact.
- Use prompts such as, "Keep looking at my eyes so you hear all of the directions/story/what I have to say," or "Help your friends talk by quietly looking at them while they talk."

LESSON 4: LOOKING TO LEARN

Introduction/Overview

The purpose of this lesson is to help the child develop a sense of visual acuity. Many children with social challenges are poor at perceiving visual details. This lesson will help them to search with their eyes in a way that will help them see the different social cues of others and learn from them. Children who have trouble with this lesson should be given extra support on clueing into the details.

Teaching Concepts

- We use our eyes to find clues in the environment.
- We look for clues about our friends and their wants and needs.
- If we miss the clues, we can pick the wrong response.

Attitude

- This is a learned behavior, and even children in a higher grade may not yet have learned this skill.
- If this is a challenge for the children, they will need more than this lesson to master the skill.
- This skill has nothing to do with how good their eyesight is or needing glasses.

Lesson Objectives

- Children will be able to find an object in a visually distracting picture.
- Children will find an object in a visually distracting room.
- Children will identify someone's attitude or emotional state by observing nonverbal cues.
- Children will identify someone's intention by observing nonverbal cues.

Lesson Introduction

Concept Map—"Looking to Learn"

Have children develop a concept map to refer to by asking them leading questions. Use the directions found in the "How to Use This Book" section.

Activities

Doggy, Where Is Your Bone?

Purpose: The children will use their eyes to look for an item in a room and concentrate on the looking process.

Figure 2.3   Looking to Learn Concept Map

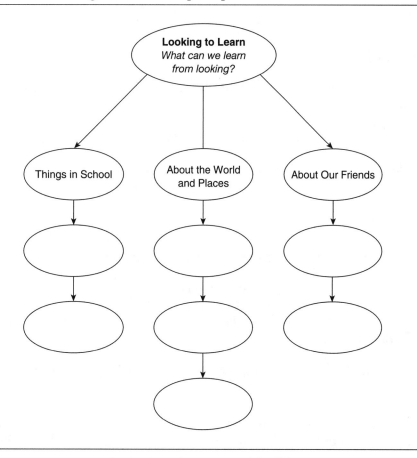

Materials: An eraser or other item to hide

Preparation: None

Procedure:

1. One child plays the part of the dog.

2. He or she sits in front of the other children with his or her back to the group.

3. The item (the bone) is put under the child's chair.

4. The rest of the children sit on the floor with their legs crossed.

5. While the "dog" is turned around with his or her eyes closed, pick someone to sneak up and steal the bone and hide it in his or her lap so it is showing slightly.

6. Then everyone says, "Doggy, doggy where is your bone? Somebody's stolen it from your home. Guess who it might be."

7. The dog has three chances to find the bone or guess who took it.

8. Sometimes the bone can be left under the dog's chair.

9. If the dog guesses right, he or she can play again.

10. If the dog is wrong, the person who had the bone is now the dog.

Emotion Bingo

Purpose: The children will be given the opportunity to look at someone's face to interpret his or her feelings.

Materials: Emotion Bingo cards found in Appendix B and bingo chips

Preparation: Make emotion cards and bingo cards from supplies in Appendix B.

Procedure:

1. Each child picks a game card and enough chips for the cards.

2. The facilitator picks an emotion card.

3. Then the facilitator uses facial expressions to describe the emotion on the card.

4. The children must match the expression with an emotion listed on their game card.

5. For younger children, overemphasize the emotion in your expression and use the more simplistic emotions cards. For older children, use a more subtle expression and include the more challenging emotion cards.

I Spy

Purpose: This activity is a fun way to get children to use eye contact and descriptive words to listen and learn.

Materials: I Spy book by Jean Marzollo, poster paper, stickers, stamps, crayons, markers, and magazine pictures used for collages

Preparation: Have supplies ready to make the poster.

Procedure:

1. Read *I Spy* to the children.

2. Have children make "I Spy" collage poster or individual pictures with stickers, magazine photos, or by drawing pictures.

3. Have each child lead an "I Spy" by giving clues for the other children to find the picture he or she is looking at. Prompt eye contact both with the picture and between children.

Friendship Cards—Using Eye Contact

Purpose: The friendship cards are used as a visual reminder for the children, to reinforce the concept that has been taught.

Materials: The following friendship cards found in Appendix A: What We Learn From Looking

Preparation: See directions in "How to Use This Book."

Procedure: See directions in "How to Use This Book."

Generalization and Consistency

- Give the children verbal prompts for all the times they need to be attentive by starting your address with, "Everyone look at my eyes so you can hear all the directions."
- Use visual prompts to assist language processing, such as holding a finger up for each direction to help the children remember.
- Use redirection phrases such as "Remember the directions," "Think about what you should be doing now," and "Think about the direction I just gave."
- Give children more specific direction when sending them to find something on their own.
- Give children visual supports, such as writing lists of directions or placing reminder cards on their desks, to help them retain directions during the day.
- Use other nonverbal forms of communication, such as facial expression, gestures, and fluctuation of tone or volume, to keep children's eye contact.
- Make sure the children are given enough time to answer questions and respond. Practice waiting twice your usual amount of time for the children to answer so they have more opportunity to process the first statement before we give them another (see "Wait Time" section in "Guidelines for Curriculum Success").

LESSON 5: INTEREST IN OTHERS

Introduction/Overview

This lesson is an opportunity for children to understand the importance of having others in their lives. The belief that all children want to interact is an incomplete idea. It is very possible that there are children you are working with who do not see the importance of other people. Traditionally, the concentration would be on why the children "feel" this way about others. In this section, we are concentrating on helping children understand the benefit and developing a concept of having others in their lives. This is also an opportunity for the teachers to get a sense of what may be challenging for each individual child when he or she is interacting.

Teaching Concepts

- Other people are fun and great to spend time with.
- Even if it may be difficult to interact with others, it has great benefits.

Attitude

- We love being with others, and we want to make more opportunities to spend time with others.
- We are nonjudgmental of those children who have difficulty with this concept.
- We believe that all children have the ability to develop these skills.

Lesson Objectives

- Children will initiate play with other children.
- Children will choose activities that include others over solitary activities.
- Children will engage in reciprocal activities with another child.
- Children will list the things that are positive about others and about spending time with others.

Lesson Introduction

Brainstorm for Key Concepts

Have children develop lists to refer to by asking them specific questions. Use the directions found in the "How to Use This Book" section. Here are some suggestions of questions to ask:

- What are the games and activities we do with others?
- What do we talk to other people about?
- How do others help us?
- Why do we have friends?

Activities

Name Ball

Purpose: This activity is just like the game of silent ball, but with an emphasis on eye contact and names. We need to make the connection for children that addressing someone must include eye contact.

Materials: Small ball, polyspots and sit-upons (if needed)

Preparation: Set up spots in a circle for children to sit on, or have the children put the spots in a circle for you.

Procedure:

1. When all children are seated, designate a child to be the starter.

2. The "starter" needs to say the name of another child, look at that child, and then throw the ball to that child.

3. If the person throwing does not look at the person he or she is throwing to, then the thrower is out. If the person being thrown to does not catch the ball, the catcher is out.

Paper Dolls

Purpose: The purpose of this activity is to have children express the qualities they like in others. It will help them to bring the things they like about others to the forefront of their minds before they get into the deeper concepts.

Materials: Paper dolls found in Appendix B, markers and crayons

Preparation: Cut out a paper doll for each child.

Procedure:

1. Use the list generated from brainstorming to help children think of ideas for things to do with friends and talk to friends about.

2. Have children draw a picture of someone who is their friend or someone they would like to be their friend.

3. Have children draw symbols or write words on the back of the doll, explaining the things they do and talk about with friends.

Who's It Going to Be?

Purpose: This activity will allow the children to think of different people to do fun activities with so they will begin to see the benefits of interacting with these people.

Materials: "Who's It Going to Be?" worksheet found in Appendix B

Preparation: Make copies of worksheet for each child.

Procedure:

1. Have children fill out the worksheet, encouraging them to think of different people for each activity listed.

2. After they have completed the sheet, have the children share their answers with the group.

Friendship Cards—Using Eye Contact

Purpose: The friendship cards are used as a visual reminder for the children, to reinforce the concept that has been taught.

Materials: The following friendship cards found in Appendix A:

- What We Do With Others
- Why We Have Friends

Preparation: See directions in "How to Use This Book."

Procedure: See directions in "How to Use This Book."

Generalization and Consistency

- Spend time following the children's lead in play and expressing your interest and enjoyment of the things they find fun. Add onto games a piece at a time and see if the children will attempt the things that you try. Cheer their exploration of new play each time they try something they have observed.
- If children are requesting a toy for themselves, ask them who they are going to play it with or prompt them to go ask a particular child.
- Celebrate every attempt and accomplishment the children make to initiate activity with others.

Being a Friend

The concept of friendship should constantly be discussed with children, as they benefit from learning the strategies needed to be a "good" friend to others. This lesson introduces the basic concepts necessary to having successful friendships. Often, children may lack the desire to have friends; sometimes friends are just too challenging and it is easier to play alone. We have to make friendship fun or the children will not see the benefit of trying. By teaching children phrases and actions that will increase their success during play, the play becomes more fun and children are then willing to try harder to build relationships with peers. The following lessons teach simple skills to the children that will help them make playing more fun.

Social Goals

- Children will engage in unstructured interactive play with similar toys with other children.
- Children will invite a peer to play.
- Children will join another child or group of children when asked to play a game or participate in an activity.
- Children will use "sweet" language to communicate with others.
- Children will follow a play theme until game or activity is finished.
- Children will use good sportsmanship in a game by cheering on a peer.

LESSON 1: FUN WITH FRIENDS

Introduction/Overview

The purpose of this lesson is to begin to lay out the basic concepts of the Wanna Play program. From this basic social structure, we branch out into all of the different concepts used in the program. We use the terms "sweet words" and "kind words" interchangeably. "Sweet words" is geared toward younger children who still interact through gross motor skills and dramatic play. "Kind words" is geared toward older elementary children who spend less of their time interacting through play. Each of the other lessons has similar interchangeable terms.

The Wanna Play program is developed to build on itself with each concept supporting the next. In each consecutive lesson, the attitudes and objectives need to be reviewed. Therefore, in this lesson and all others, eye contact and interaction need to be continually reinforced on a daily basis.

Teaching Concepts

- Components that go into being a friend are introduced.
- Having friends and being friends are important in our lives.
- It is important to choose positive words and actions every time we play and interact with others.
- Everyone needs to have the skills to interact with others in a positive way.

Attitude

- Play is fun and we believe you can do it.
- Even though this may be hard for children with developmental disorders, we still need to teach it until they learn it because they *can* learn it.

Lesson Objective

- Children will be introduced to the beginning concepts of play that are coming up in the next lessons.
- Children will be introduced to the idea that play is an activity that involves others.

Lesson Introduction

Brainstorm for Key Concepts

Have children develop lists to refer to by asking them specific questions. Use the directions found in the "How to Use This Book" section. Here are some suggestions for questions to ask:

- Who are your friends? (Allow children to include parents, cousins, and other family members.)
- What do we do with friends?
- Why we have friends and other people in our lives.
- What do you do to be a good friend? (Give examples of traits if they are stuck. Also, use the list of specific people to help them come up with adjectives.)

Activities

Friendship Poster

Purpose: This activity will help the children make a visual reminder of who their friends are and things they like to do with friends.

Materials: Large paper for poster, 8½ × 11 paper, markers or crayons, glue sticks, construction paper (optional)

Preparation: None

Procedure:

1. Have children draw a picture of themselves and a friend doing something together. If it isn't clear what the picture is of, ask the child who it is and what they are doing, and then label the picture for them.

2. The children can then cut out the picture and glue it on construction paper or directly on the poster.

3. Label the top of the poster "Fun With Friends."

Friendship Train

Purpose: The Friendship Train activity can be adapted to teach many different friend concepts. The questions asked of the children can be modified to fit the friend concept that is appropriate for the group or child.

Materials: Friendship Train coloring sheets found in Appendix B, crayons or markers

Preparation: Make copies of Friendship Train coloring sheets and gather supplies.

Procedure:

1. Ask the children the friendship question that is appropriate for their age or level of concept development. Examples: "What do you like to do with your friends?" or "Who are your friends?" or just list the names of the children and have it be a train of the friends in the class.

2. Either have the children write the answer on the train or write it for them.

3. The children can then color the train, cut it out, and glue it onto construction paper.

4. Photographs of the children can be added to their train if available.

5. Hang the train pictures around the room to help remind the children of who their friends are in the group.

Friendship Cards—Being a Friend

Purpose: The friendship cards are used as a visual reminder for the children, to reinforce the concept that has been taught.

Materials: The following friendship card found in Appendix A:

- What Do You Do to Be a Good Friend?

Preparation: See directions in "How to Use This Book."

Procedure: See directions in "How to Use This Book."

Consistency and Generalization

- Pick a social situation (e.g., a birthday party) and have the children draw pictures of themselves at the event.
- If children are not doing representational drawing, have them color in pictures of children playing.
- Celebrate children's attempts to initiate play or join others in play activities.
- Ask open-ended questions about children's play experiences when you were not with them.
- Use the word "friend" whenever possible when describing peers together.

LESSON 2: SWEET WORDS/KIND WORDS

Introduction/Overview

This lesson addresses the importance of positive, proactive speech, which we will call "sweet words." As immature as the phrase may seem, we have attempted different phrases and "sweet words" is the one children seem to remember the best over time. The phrase refers to both the language with which we choose to communicate and the tone of voice we adopt. For some groups, whining, grumpy, or brusque tones of voice are not an issue. However, we suggest helping children identify what this sounds like when others use it and ways of avoiding using these tones.

Teaching Concepts

- The best way to communicate is with a positive affect.
- We get more of what we want if we stay calm and positive.
- The way we speak to people helps them to know what kind of person we are.
- Sweet/kind words go with any emotion.

- Sometimes being sweet is just being calm and nonjudgmental.
- Kind words are the best way to get what we want.
- People are more willing to help when we treat them kindly.
- Friends are more willing to be with us if we are kind.
- Using sweet/kind words will tell people how we want to be treated.

Attitude

- Use it or lose it: if we don't model it consistently, the children will not use the positive language.
- Make it big enough to notice: many children need us to overemphasize the positive tones and language in order for them to understand the difference between what we are saying and what they are using.

Lesson Objective

- Children will identify positive language and phrases that they can use in everyday situations as well as conflict situations with their peers.
- Children will use sweet/kind words when communicating with others.

Lesson Introduction

Brainstorm for Key Concepts

Have children develop lists to refer to by asking them specific questions. Use the directions found in the "How to use this book" section. Here are some suggestions for questions to ask:

- What are sweet/kind words?
- What are some sweet words that you know? Examples: Please, Thank you, You're welcome, I'm sorry, May I . . . ?, Will you please . . . ?
- Who would we use our sweet words with?
- Why do we use sweet words and sweet voices with our friends?

Activities

Sweet Words Mobile

Purpose: Make a mobile of the words children use to be sweet/kind. This is a good opportunity to test the retention of the students.

Materials: Paper for writing words, hole punch, string, paper plates or hangers

Preparation: Copy words for children to color in and cut out.

Procedure:

1. Use children's brainstormed sweet words to make bubble words (words with outlines of the letters for the children to color in).

2. Have children color in the words and cut out the letters.

3. Punch holes in the tops of the letters.

4. Make a separate mobile for each word.

5. Hang letters from a paper plate or hanger.

Making Phrases Sweeter

Purpose: To analyze the phrases that we use and hear and find out if they are "sweet words" and if they can be improved upon.

Materials: Poster/easel paper, markers for teacher, crayons or markers for children

Preparation: Make a list of words and phrases used by the children or by their favorite cartoon or other characters. Write them out on a poster for the children. Use words or phrases the children have used or ones that can be found in current culture including popular cartoons.

Procedure:

1. Show children the poster and read aloud the list of words and phrases.

2. Have children go and identify which are phrased as "sweet words" and which are not.

3. As a class or in small groups, have the children rephrase the words to make them "sweet words."

Role-Play With Friends

Purpose: To have children act out and practice the social skills taught.

Materials: Situation cards found in Appendix B, paper bags for puppets, markers or crayons

Preparation: Cut out the situation cards. Have children make paper bag puppets of themselves.

Procedure:

1. Based on the situation cards, decide the sweet words you need.

2. Have children volunteer to role-play using the situation cards provided. Each child takes a turn playing a character and playing him- or herself.

3. Have the audience reflect and brainstorm other things that could have been said.

Drawing With Limited Materials

Purpose: Creates a need to communicate and request things using sweet words.

Materials: Crayons or markers, large paper

Preparation: Remind children about sweet words and how we use them when we are working together. Write sweet words from brainstormed list in bubble letters on the large white paper.

Procedure:

1. Create a poster of some of the sweet words the children have brainstormed, writing them in bubble letters for the children to fill in.

2. Have limited markers/crayons on the table to encourage the children to request them from one another.

Topple by Pressman Toy Co.

Purpose: This is a great game to use to help children use sweet words in the contexts of turn taking. There is a fine motor challenge imbedded in the game that needs to be kept in mind.

Materials: Topple game

Preparation: See directions in Topple game.

Procedure:

1. Play the game according to the rules or have the children brainstorm new or additional rules first, write them down, and play by those rules.

2. Concentrate on the positive words used during the game.

3. Focus on pointing out how the children respond to friends during the game.

Mother, May I?

Purpose: Verbal game of requesting. The competition of these games will affect the attitude of the participants.

Materials: None

Preparation: None

Procedure:

1. Line children up side by side on one end of the room/playground.

2. One student (or the teacher) plays the "mother" and stands a good distance away from the others. "Mother" addresses the first student,

saying something like "Mary, you may take 3 giant steps." Mary must then say, "Mother, may I?" If she remembers to do so, Mother says, "Yes, you may," and Mary takes the steps forward. If she forgets to ask using her sweet words, she has to go back to the start.

3. The first child to reach Mother wins.

4. Give children behavior-specific feedback on how well they requested with sweet words.

Friendship Cards—Being a Friend

Purpose: The friendship cards are used as a visual reminder for the children, to reinforce the concept that has been taught.

Materials: The following friendship cards found in Appendix A:

- Sweet Words You Can Use
- Why We Use Sweet/Kind Words With Our Friends

Preparation: See directions in "How to Use This Book."

Procedure: See directions in "How to Use This Book."

Generalization and Consistency

Developing a Positive Affect

These are the terms used when discussing positive behavior with the child:

> Sweet words/kind words—polite language
>
> Sweet voice/kind voice—kind tone of voice

- Celebrate every attempt children make to use positive, proactive language.
- Prompt sweet/kind words and voices for children. Initially, give the phrases or model the voice that is more positive. Transition to just asking the child to try it again.
- When the children choose to whine, complain, or pout as a means of responding to not getting their way, little to no emotional response should be given. Tell them you do not understand them when they choose these behaviors. Explain what their choices are, how to accept what is being offered, and how to attempt a new positive way to get what they want, or else continue to be unhappy—the choice is up to them. Then walk away.
- Use these phrases in everyday activity to help remind children to use sweet words:

> "Say it with your sweet words."
>
> "Say it again with a sweet voice."
>
> "Say it again with a calm voice."

- Use behavior-specific feedback to help children see how and when they are using this type of communication:

  "Thank you for asking with sweet words."

  "I appreciate you using sweet words."

  "Those sweet words really make me want to help you."

  "Because you used your sweet words, your friends want to play with/help you."

LESSON 3: SAFE BODY/BODY SAFETY

Introduction/Overview

Children's ability to have an awareness of their body space can be challenged by sensory needs that may not even be diagnosed. Children frequently are not cognizant of how close they are to another person. Also, children with social challenges use physical actions to attempt to interact when they do not know what else to do; physical humor is easy to use and can get more attention from peers. All of the aforementioned possibilities impede the children's ability to choose appropriate body actions. The following activities will begin to teach children how to safely use their body.

Teaching Concepts

- Safety is the only way to be friendly.
- Our friend's safety is more important than being funny.
- Using our words, not our bodies, helps to get us what we want.
- We need to use our eyes to see where our bodies are.
- We need to practice controlling our impulses.
- Toys are to be used in a safe way.

Attitude

- Children use acts of physical force when they don't have the words to use.
- Children need to be taught to use words instead of being punished for actions.
- Children need to be shown how to safely use their bodies.

Lesson Objectives

- Children will respect the personal space of peers and adults.
- Children will ask before they touch, hug, or hold the hand of a peer or adult.
- Children will begin a conversation with a peer or adult, instead of hugging them to begin a social interaction.
- Children will use appropriate levels of movement and energy for different activities and environments.

Lesson Introduction

Brainstorm for Key Concepts

Have children develop lists to refer to by asking them specific questions. Use the directions found in the "How to Use This Book" section. Here are some suggestions for questions to ask, along with key concepts to discuss:

- Why do we keep our body safe?
- Why do we keep our friend's body safe?
- How do we use our hands and have a safe body?

    Gentle hands vs. hitting hands

    Keep hands to ourselves vs. hands on our friends

- How do we use our feet and have a safe body?

    Walking feet vs. running feet

    Keep feet to ourselves vs. putting our feet on our friends

- Do we sit next to our friends or on top of our friends?
- Do we stand too close or keep a safe distance?

If children use "don'ts" (don't hit) change the don'ts into "do's." Children need to learn what to do. They know what not to do.

Activities

Making Safe Bodies

Purpose: Teach children what to do using a visual representation of it.

Materials: Safe Body outlines found in Appendix B, and markers or crayons

Preparation: Make copies of the body outlines for each child.

Procedure:

1. Have the children color in a body outline and make it into a friend by naming it.

2. Help the children name each body part with the safe body parts list from the Lesson Introduction.

3. Label the body parts for them.

4. Hang the colored-in body outlines in the room as a visual, and use them to remind children of safe body choices.

Musical Islands

Purpose: Continue to increase the children's awareness of where their body is in relation to others.

Materials: Polyspots, music, CD player

Preparation: None

Procedure:

1. Place polyspots on the floor and have the children stand around them.

2. Play music and have the children dance around the spots.

3. When the music stops, have each child jump onto a spot.

4. Before the next round, remove 1–2 spots.

5. When there are fewer spots than children, the children are to begin to share spots. Remind them about keeping their friends' bodies safe when they are on the spots.

6. The goal is for all the children to place one foot on one spot when the music stops, keeping check on their bodies.

Safe Body Puzzle

Purpose: Another activity to help teach children what to do by giving them a visual representation of it.

Materials: Safe Body and cutout clothes found in Appendix B, markers, glue

Preparation: Make copies of the body outlines and cutout clothes (decide if you want to have the children cut out the clothes or if you should give them to them cut out already).

Procedure:

1. Have each child make the body into a friend by naming it.

2. Help the children name each body part with the safe body parts list in the Lesson Introduction.

3. Label the body parts for them. Write the safe body parts on the clothes so the children can glue them onto their safe body.

4. Children can then color in the rest of the body.

5. Hang the dressed and colored-in body outlines in the room as a visual and use them to remind children of safe body choices.

Foot Loose by Interactive Playthings

Purpose: Increases the children's awareness of how their body moves and how to switch from one movement to another.

Materials: Foot Loose game

Preparation: See Foot Loose game.

Procedure:

1. Play the game according to the rules on the game or have the children brainstorm new or additional rules first, write them down, and play by those rules.

2. Help the children build awareness of how much space they will need around their body before they do the exercise.

3. Point out the different body movements during each exercise.

Balloon Keep Up

Purpose: To build the children's awareness of where their body is in relation to others.

Materials: Blown-up balloons

Preparation: None

Procedure:

1. Have children stand in a group in a large space.

2. The object of the game is to keep tapping the balloon into the air without letting it drop on the ground.

3. Remind children that they need to stay on their feet and keep their friends' bodies safe.

4. Use the brainstormed list again to remind them what body safety is.

5. Continue to increase the children's awareness of where their body is in relation to others.

Parachute Keep Up

Purpose: Continue to increase the children's awareness of where their body is in relation to others. The activity also helps children begin to work as a group and observe others' movements in order to move with them.

Materials: Parachute, beanbag or small stuffed animal to toss in the air

Preparation: None

Procedure:

1. Have children stand in a circle and hold one or two handles of the parachute depending on its size.

2. Put the beanbag or stuffed animal in the center of the parachute.

3. The object is to have all the children throw the beanbag into the air in one motion and then catch it with the parachute.

4. Count to see how many times you can catch it as a group.

5. When it drops, have the children try again and try to beat their score as a group.

Friendship Cards—Being a Friend

Purpose: The friendship cards are used as a visual reminder for the children, to reinforce the concept that has been taught.

Materials: The following friendship cards found in Appendix A:

- Why We Keep Our Bodies Safe
- Why We Keep Our Friends' Bodies Safe
- How We Use Our Hands/Feet
- How We Use Our Bodies

Preparation: See directions in "How to Use This Book."

Procedure: See directions in "How to Use This Book."

Generalization and Consistency

- If the children choose to sit on, touch, tackle, or hug someone without asking, they have chosen to move away from the activity.

    1. Convey to children that they need to ask first for it to be ok.

    2. If the children choose to ask first, say no, and offer an appropriate behavior. Example: hold hands or sit next to you.

- Giving the children suggestions of sensory intervention during moments of high challenge aids them in resolution.

LESSON 4: PLAYING TOGETHER

Introduction/Overview

The goal of this lesson is to help the children learn to respect their friends and the toys during play and still have fun. The term "share" is constantly used to teach children to have successful interactions during play. Sharing is a conceptual idea, lacking definitive time components. Children will more easily learn this idea if the facilitator uses the phrase "take turns." Taking turns has a defined beginning and end and allows the person facilitating to give countdowns to alert the children about their turn. Children should also be given the choice of whether or not to bring out their own toys to share. It is all right to keep special toys for themselves. Children should be told before the play begins that if they bring out the toy or bring the toy to school, they will need to take turns. If they do not want to take turns, then they can leave the toy at home.

Teaching Concepts

- Respect others' creations and toys.
- Everyone has a right to keep his or her things safe.
- We show our friends we care by taking care of their things.
- Respect how others choose to play.
- We only add to someone's creation or game when invited.
- Our friends may disagree with us and that's okay.
- Everyone has the right to have fun.
- Everyone has the right to play his or her own way.

Attitude

- Not all choices children make during play seem fair to us or other children.
- When children are having fun, they may need positive reminders to make the best choices.

Lesson Objectives

- Children will physically show appreciation of others by including others and taking turns.
- Children will choose to play a friend's game or finish an activity that a friend wants to finish.
- Children will teach a friend to play a game.
- Children will try a new game to have fun.
- Children will attempt to join another child or group of children in play.

Lesson Introduction

Concept Map—"What Do We Need to Do to Play Together and Have Fun?"

Have children develop a concept map to refer to by asking them leading questions. Use the directions found in the "How to Use This Book" section.

Figure 3.1   Play Together

Activities

Centers

Purpose: To allow children to try new activities and interact with other children participating in the activity.

Materials: Select toys/games that are age appropriate and offer the children a chance to interact while they play. Buckets of cars and legos are usually great ideas as are card games or toys with limited numbers of pieces.

Preparation: Arrange the toys/games in separate areas with enough space for the children to comfortably play.

Procedure:

1. Group the children in equal numbers, also considering the dynamic and personalities of the group and how much social challenge specific children can handle.

2. Explain that the children will have a certain amount of time with each toy or game and then they will switch. Try to give the children equal time with each center.

3. Prompt with a 2-minute countdown before switching.

4. During the playtime, facilitate from afar if possible. Look for opportunities to prompt what they have learned in the previous lessons. This is a great time to encourage the use of sweet words, safe distance, and positive friendship skills.

5. Acknowledge all attempts by the children to interact positively with their friends.

Teach a Friend a Game

Purpose: To help children attempt beginning leadership skills and manage their temptation to overuse their knowledge when explaining the directions.

Materials: Whatever games the children bring in. Help the parent by giving guidelines for an appropriate game: The game should be able to include "___" number of players, and the children should have played the game enough to be comfortable explaining it to others.

Preparation: None

Procedure:

1. Have the children take turns bringing in a game from home to teach their friends. If it is a group larger than four children, break into smaller groups and have one child from each group bring in a game.

2. Send a note home reminding the parents and instructing them that the game should be one that the children can play easily. The parents should not need to provide any additional instruction.

3. Before the children begin teaching their friends to play, remind the group of the things they have learned about being good friends. Review briefly the concepts in this unit that would be beneficial in this situation and for the group.

4. Facilitate as needed. The intention is to have the children be as independent as possible. Let the child finish the explanation once and then ask the group if they have any questions.

5. Let the child attempt to answer the questions first. If some additional support is needed, give a brief instruction or two and then let them begin playing. Again, facilitate as needed.

6. Reinforce the concept by commending the children for bringing the game to teach their friends.

7. If the children in the group need more visual support for following directions, write the directions on a list to be visible as the children play the game.

Building With Friends

Purpose: Construct a play environment that requires positive interactions to have fun.

Materials: Blocks or legos, a hoop or tape circle on the floor

Preparation: None

Procedure:

1. Divide children into groups of four or less.

2. Explain that they are to build a specific construction (based on children's common interest) within the area (hoop) with the blocks or legos you give them.

3. Facilitate as needed with prompts and reminders for positive interactions and problem solving.

Friendship Cards—Being a Friend

Purpose: The friendship cards are used as a visual reminder for the children, to reinforce the concept that is being taught.

Materials: The following friendship card found in Appendix A

- What We Do Together to Play and Have Fun

Preparation: See directions in "How to Use This Book."

Procedure: See directions in "How to Use This Book."

Generalization and Consistency

- Continue to strengthen the children's ability to take turns; suggest trades, substituting a new toy and time-sharing if there is a conflict situation.
- When the children choose not to play friendly, remind them that they have now made the choice not to play and need to move away from the game until the game is over.
- If the children are requesting a toy for themselves, ask them who they are going to play it with or prompt them to go to ask a particular child to join them.
- Being a friend—Reinforce the concepts of following the directions, using a kind attitude, letting someone take his or her turn, keeping the game together when it needs to be, and coming to agreements.
- This is the time to set the rule in the classroom that choosing not to play friendly is choosing not to play.

Appropriate Body Behavior

Introduction/Overview

In many situations when a child is having difficulty making friends or behaving appropriately in a social setting, the problem is rooted in the child's body awareness and sensory regulation. Many children have the interest and desire to interact with others but have difficultly doing so because they are unaware of the appropriate way to behave and use their bodies.

Social Goals

- Children will respect personal space of peers and adults by standing at appropriate distances during interaction.
- Children will use sensory suggestions when prompted by an adult or, when needed, without prompting.
- Children will ask before they touch, hug, or hold the hand of a peer or adult.
- Children will initiate a conversation or social interaction with a peer or adult using appropriate physical contact.
- Children will use appropriate levels of movement and energy for different activities and environments.

LESSON 1: INTRODUCTION TO APPROPRIATE BODY BEHAVIOR

Introduction/Overview

The main purpose of this lesson is to review the safe body concepts that were introduced in Unit 3, "Being a Friend." We want the children to build on the concepts that they've learned in previous lessons and to expand their understanding that social skills do not exist in a vacuum but are interconnected. Reintroducing the body safety concepts will help the children establish the foundation of social interaction. We can then build on the concept of interaction and introduce the next level of social complexity.

Teaching Concepts

- We need to have a safe body when playing with our friends.
- We need to move at certain speeds in different situations to help keep our friends safe.
- People want to spend more time with us when we keep our bodies clean and dressed.

Attitude

- Certain activities in this lesson, if not performed with care, can damage the children's body image, so we must always choose our words carefully.
- Being comfortable and positive when talking about sensitive issues will help children to develop an openness about image issues.

Lesson Objectives

- Children will be introduced to the concept of appropriate body and be prepared for the lessons that follow.

Lesson Introduction

Brainstorm for Key Concepts

Have children develop lists to refer to by asking them specific questions. Use the directions found in the "How to Use This Book" section. Here are some suggestions for questions to ask:

- What does it mean to have an appropriate body?
- What do we do to use a safe body?

Activities

Body Outline Poster

Purpose: This is a fun activity to introduce the unit. It gives the children opportunities for self-expression. It also gives the adult a look into the children's self-image and body concept.

Materials: Large roll of paper or butcher paper, markers/crayons, lots of space

Preparation: Cut a long piece of paper for each child.

Procedure:

1. Have children get into pairs.

2. Have one child lie on the floor and the other child trace his or her outline onto the large paper. Then have the children switch so each child has an outline of his or her body.

3. Have the children make the bodies look like themselves. Instruct them to draw their face and the clothes they like to wear.

4. Have children write three or four words from the concept development list on the posters, above the pictures of their bodies.

5. For younger children, write the words and the terms from the concept development list for them in bubble letters.

Mirror Game

Purpose: In this game, each child must use his or body in sync with another child. It gives the children the opportunity to have to regulate their movements in coordination with someone else. Even when they want to move fast, they need to follow the other child.

Materials: Polyspots or construction paper taped to the ground (optional)

Preparation: None

Procedure:

1. Divide children into pairs.

2. Have children face each other sitting cross-legged on the floor.

3. Have the children decide who will be the mirror in each pair.

4. Instruct the children that the "mirror" child will need to copy whatever movements the other child is making.

5. After a few minutes, have the children stand (use spots to help kids stay in place if needed) and play again while standing. Encourage the children to use their whole bodies.

Human Obstacle Course

Purpose: In this game, children will be the obstacle course as well as go through it. They will need to be careful of their friends and use appropriate behavior to get through the course correctly.

Materials: Open safe space, polyspots or construction paper taped to the ground or sit-upons, optional balls

Preparation: None

Procedure:

1. Split the children into two groups.

2. Tell the groups that they will take turns *being* an obstacle course and going through one.

3. Have one group sit and wait while the other group finds a spot for each child.

4. Ask the children in the obstacle course group to decide what obstacle they would each like to be.

5. Make suggestions if children are having trouble coming up with ideas (tell them to be something people have to crawl under or something people need to jump over; children can use balls if they want to be human basketball hoops by making their arms into a circle "hoop").

6. Explain how to go through the course (example: "First go to Jen and jump over her, then go to Mike and shoot the ball through his arms like it's a basketball").

7. Have the other group of children go through the course one at a time. Remind them to use their bodies appropriately.

8. Switch groups and have the other children make a new course.

Hula Hoop

Purpose: This activity gives children a chance to move their bodies at different speeds and in different directions.

Materials: Hula Hoops (one for each child), music that goes at different speeds (rock and roll to classical)

Preparation: Put Hula Hoops on the ground spaced far enough apart that children will not bump into one another.

Procedure:

1. Have every child choose a hoop and sit in the middle of it.

2. Explain that the object of the game is to follow the music and directions the best that they can.

3. Put one speed of music on and give movement direction to kids such as

   – Jump in and out
   – Run around outside of hoop
   – Run around inside the hoop
   – Walk around with one foot inside and one foot outside

4. Try the same movements with a different speed of music.

Relay Race

Purpose: This gives the children the chance to use a multitude of skills. In this case, they will be asked to concentrate on using appropriate body movements to complete the tasks and keep everyone safe.

Materials: Spoons, golf balls, pom-pom balls, balloons

Preparation: Split the children into teams and set up the course. Determine the size and makeup of the teams based on the needs of your group.

Procedure:

1. Each child needs to run down and back with the ball on the spoon without dropping the ball. If the ball is dropped, the child has to start over.

2. Start with the heaviest ball (it will stay on the spoon the best).

3. With each race, introduce a new ball or the balloon.

4. Remind the children that they need to pay attention to their bodies, and comment if someone becomes too crazy or wild and needs to gain some control.

5. Also point out when someone is going too slowly and can speed up.

6. Run relay races.

Friendship Cards—Appropriate Body

Purpose: The friendship cards are used as a visual reminder for the children, to reinforce the concept that has been taught.

Materials: The following friendship card found in Appendix A:

- Appropriate Body

Preparation: See directions in "How to Use This Book."

Procedure: See directions in "How to Use This Book."

LESSON 2: BODY NEEDS—STRENGTHS AND WEAKNESSES

Introduction/Overview

The goal of this lesson is to help the children develop an understanding of their body needs. We caution adults to be aware of whether they are using this to develop a "belief of inability." We want this lesson to be about achieving instead of limiting. That is why we want to develop the concept of needing help instead of weakness. We want the children to understand that need is not equal to deficiency. We also want the children to develop the desire to achieve things on their own.

Teaching Concepts

- We can all do active things.
- We can all learn to do things on our own.
- Sometimes we need help and that is okay.

Attitude

- Many people do not take the time to think about their strengths.
- We can make up for our weakness by using our strengths.

Lesson Objective

- Children will identify their body abilities.
- Children will identify the activities they enjoy.
- Children will identify those activities with which they need help.
- Children will identify their friends' body abilities.
- Children will modify games to meet their friends' needs.

Lesson Introduction

Brainstorm for Key Concepts

Have children develop lists to refer to by asking them specific questions. Use the directions found in the "How to Use This Book" section. Here are some suggestions of questions to ask:

- What are some activities you do well?
- What are some things with which you need help?
- Where are some places you go to get help?

Activities

Body Strengths and Weaknesses Collage

Purpose: In this activity, the children will make a visual representation of what they were discussing above. The intention is to help them create a positive attitude toward their own challenges.

Materials: Two large posters, crayons, markers, glue, construction paper, white drawing paper

Preparation: Label the top of one poster "Things We Do Well" and the other "Getting Help."

Procedure:

1. Have each child draw one picture of him- or herself doing something the child does well and one of someone helping him or her with something that is a challenge.

2. Have each child cut out the pictures, attach them to a construction paper backing, and put them on the appropriate poster.

3. When posters are finished, have children volunteer to share what they drew and explain how they feel when someone helps them.

Spot Twister

Purpose: In this game, children will move their bodies in odd, contorted ways to reach the spots on the ground. It will give the children an opportunity to see what they can and cannot do. It will also show the children the physical limitations of their friends. This is a great way to show that physical limitations do not mean a lack of fun.

Materials: Polyspots

Preparation: Lay out the colored spots in random places around the play area so they are within reaching distance of each other.

Procedure:

1. Have each child start out on a spot.

2. Explain to the children that you will call out three colors and they will need to have at least one body part on each color. For more challenged groups, only do two colors at a time.

3. As the children are getting on the colors, make suggestions of how to move their bodies to help them reach the spots.

4. Make it more challenging by naming a specific body part they have to use for a particular color.

Disability Obstacle Course

Purpose: In this activity, the children will go through a simple obstacle course but will do it with a new physical challenge.

Materials: Scarves, gross motor equipment, tape, index cards

Preparation: Write challenges on the cards, one for each child (examples: can't see, only one leg, broken arm, can't talk).

Procedure:

1. Have children use the equipment to make an obstacle course for themselves.

2. After course is finished, have the children pick a challenge from the deck of cards.

3. Use the scarves and the tape and help the children to challenge themselves by tying arms to their bodies, legs together, or by covering eyes or mouth.

4. Split children into groups or pairs and give them a few minutes to think about and discuss how they are going to help each other.

5. Have the children go through the obstacle course.

6. After they go through the course, have the children take some time to discuss the experience. Point out that helping others when they need it is an important part of playing games with friends.

Problem-Solving Game

Purpose: The purpose of this game is to have the children remake the games so that everyone can play and be involved.

Materials: A few games (boards games, gross motor, and art activities), poster board, and markers

Preparation: Pick the games with which you know some of the children have difficulty. Write the names of the games, one on each poster board.

Procedure:

1. Talk about what we have learned about the needs of our friends.

2. Have the children review their needs and things they have learned about making things accessible for everyone.

3. Show the games you have picked.

4. Go through each game and have the children share what they or a friend of theirs would have trouble with in each game. (Example: "My sister can't play that game because she can't read.") List the challenges on the posters with the game names.

5. After getting a list of three or four challenges for each game, go back and brainstorm with the children how they could change the game so that everyone can play. (Example: Use memory picture cards instead of words cards for someone who can't read.)

6. Have the children play one of the games in the new, modified way.

7. Have children come back in a discussion group and talk about whether it was fun or if something new should be tried.

8. Finish by sharing that even the adaptive way of doing things can be fun.

Friendship Cards—Appropriate Body

Purpose: The friendship cards are used as a visual reminder for the children, to reinforce the concept that has been taught.

Materials: The following friendship cards found in Appendix A:

- Things I Do Well
- Things I Need Help With
- People Who Help Me

Preparation: See directions in "How to Use This Book."

Procedure: See directions in "How to Use This Book."

LESSON 3: PERSONAL PLAY SPACE

Introduction/Overview

This lesson is designed to help children understand that there are invisible bubbles around them and around other people, which are defined as personal space. We want to give the children an understanding of this invisible space and have a sensory experience that will support this concept. Children with social challenges have difficulty noticing the nonverbal body language cues that are the key to social awareness. They will not notice when people may think they are standing too close. Because of this, children will invade their peers' personal body space without realizing it. In this lesson, the goal is to illustrate to the child what personal body space is and what can happen if it is not respected.

Teaching Concepts

- Everyone has a different personal space bubble.
- Not everyone has the ability to perceive other people's personal space.

Attitude

- Not everyone has the same body needs and sensitivities.
- Everyone has a different comfort level when it comes to personal space.

Lesson Objectives

- Children will have a physical experience of their own personal space.
- Children will identify the appropriate personal physical space needed in relationships with various people.
- Children will learn and use strategies to regulate personal space.

Lesson Introduction

Brainstorm for Key Concepts

Have children develop lists to refer to by asking them specific questions. Use the directions found in the "How to Use This Book" section. Here are some suggestions of questions to ask:

- What is personal space?
- When do we need to check personal space?
- Have you ever had someone come into your personal space? What happened? How did it feel?
- What do we say if someone is in our personal space?

Activities

Making Our Own Personal Space Circle

Purpose: This activity is designed to help children have a physical experience of what personal space is and what their comfort level is. The activity will add a visual aspect to the concept of personal space.

Materials: Poster board (one for each child), various colored markers

Preparation: Draw an X in the center of each poster. Find a space so that all of the posters can be laid out on the floor.

Procedure:

1. Have the children each take a turn standing on an X in the middle of the poster.

2. Have each child draw a circle around him- or herself that will be that child's personal space.

3. Have the rest of the class line up on the edge of the circle and ask the child if he or she feels comfortable or if he or she needs to have the group step back.

4. Have the child draw a new circle for the class to stand at the edge of.

5. Repeat the process with each child.

6. Compare the circles.

7. Save circles for activities in next lesson.

Personal Space Freeze Dance

Purpose: In this activity, children will experience how difficult it is to keep appropriate personal space when involved in an active game. It will give them the opportunity to check their personal space often while in an activity.

Materials: Polyspots, masking tape, CD player, music CDs

Preparation: Put spots down on the ground in a random pattern, with a few more spots than there are children. Make sure some of the spots are close to each other and others are spaced well apart.

Procedure:

1. Have all children get on a spot and have each child check to make sure that no one is in his or her personal space.

2. Instruct the children that they will play a freeze dance. When the music starts, they are to dance around the spots and when the music stops, they need to get on a spot.

3. Play music and stop after a short time.

4. Ask all the children to look and see if anyone is too close to them. If a child thinks someone is too close, have him or her move, or have the child ask the person who is too close to move to another spot using sweet words.

Friendship Cards—Appropriate Body

Purpose: The friendship cards are used as a visual reminder for the children, to reinforce the concept that has been taught.

Materials: The following friendship cards found in Appendix A:

- My Personal Space
- What We Say If Someone Is in Our Personal Space

Preparation: See directions in "How to Use This Book."

Procedure: See directions in "How to Use This Book."

Generalization and Consistency

- Use sit-upons, polyspots, or other mats when children are sitting on the floor to help them space themselves appropriately.
- If a child invades a peer's body space, point out the person's facial and body expressions to help the child see the cues that tell him or her to back up.
- Giving suggestions of sensory input when the child is overwhelmed to help him or her calm down and move through space in a safer way.

LESSON 4: BODY PRIVACY

Introduction/Overview

In this lesson, we will discuss body privacy, both our own and that of our friends. We chose to separate this from personal play space in order to give it the attention it deserves. Many children, with disabilities and without, fall victim to inappropriate touching by adults and even other children. Many children with disabilities get labeled as physically aggressive simply because they have never been properly taught appropriate body behavior. We want to empower children by educating them as to what is safe and appropriate when interacting with others and what to do when things cross the line of appropriate behavior. In this and the next lesson, our intention is to avoid shame as much as possible in order to make sure the children do not develop poor body concepts. We will discuss how to keep our own body private and how to respect others' body privacy. We will also address safety and what it means, and what to do when someone uses inappropriate touch.

Teaching Concepts

- Our body is our own, and we keep it to ourselves.
- Our friends' bodies are private, and we respect that by using our hands appropriately.
- We tell Mom, Dad, and doctors when someone touches us inappropriately and where.

Attitude

- Our comfort with the subject makes a very big impact on how the children will react to the information.
- We need to be comfortable with discussing sensitive topics.
- This is a positive opportunity, and we should be excited to help our children be safe.

Lesson Objective

- Children will identify the areas of the body that are private.
- Children will identify and use appropriate forms of touch with others.
- Children will identify what to do if their own body privacy is invaded.

Lesson Introduction

Concept Map—"Body Privacy"

Have children develop a concept map to refer to by asking them leading questions. Use the directions found in the "How to Use This Book" section.

Activities

Appropriate Pyramids

Purpose: This is a visual exercise to help illustrate the "privacy level" for different parts of the body. We need to focus on the positive aspect of keeping our bodies private and safe.

Materials: Pyramids (see Appendix B), markers, poster

Preparation: Make a copy of pyramid for each child. Make large poster of pyramid.

Figure 4.1 Body Privacy Concept Map

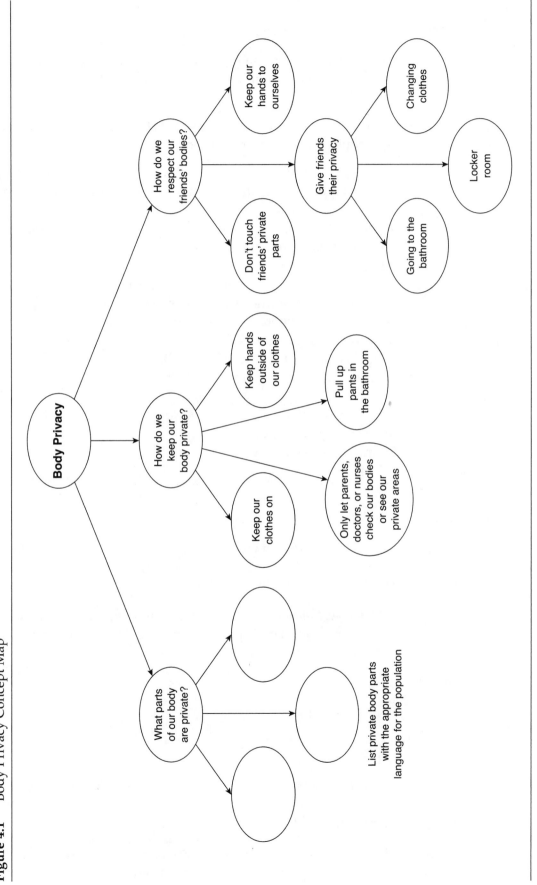

Procedure:

1. Brainstorm a list of people in the children's lives.

2. Introduce the different categories of people in the Appropriate Pyramid and have the children give examples of the people they know in each category.

3. Write on poster the appropriate behaviors that children can do with these groups of people. Here are some examples:

    a. Parents/Doctor/Grandparents—kiss, hug, sit on lap, get help getting dressed or undressed, have them check private areas, talk to

    b. Teacher/Nurse—Go to for help with body issues when sick, get help in the bathroom, put arm around, give high five, hold hand, talk to

    c. Aunts/Uncle /Cousins/Brother/Sister—hug, kiss on cheek, ask to get parent when need help with body issue, get help with clothes or bath when parent says it is ok, put arm around, give high five, hold hand, talk to

    d. School friends/Family friends/Close neighbors—put arm around, give high five, hold hand, wave to, say "Hi," go to in an emergency, talk to

    e. Community helpers/Other neighbors—wave to, say "Hi," go to in an emergency, talk to

    f. Strangers—smile, say "hi"

4. Have children fill in one or two answers on their own pyramids.

What's Missing?—Dress-Up Game

Purpose: In this activity, children will use dolls to practice appropriate dress.

Materials: Dress-up dolls, doll clothes, basket

Preparation: Make bags of outfits with one item missing; put missing items in basket. Dress each doll inappropriately, both putting clothes on wrong and forgetting to cover private body parts.

Procedure:

1. Split children into groups and give each team a doll.

2. Have the groups share what they observe to be wrong with the way the dolls are dressed.

3. Hand out bags of clothes and have children redress dolls appropriately.

Question Scavenger Hunt

Purpose: This activity is a fun way to test how well the children retained the information in the concept map in the lesson introduction. It is a combination of quiz game and scavenger hunt.

Materials: Two large posters, each with an outline of a body; two sets of clothing cut out to fit the bodies on the posters (use "Safe Body" and "Safe Body Clothes" worksheets in Appendix B as guides); index cards; questions based on the concept map

Preparation: Make the posters and clothes. Write questions based on the answers the group came up with for the concept map on the index cards. Hide the clothes for the posters around the room.

Procedure:

1. Split the class into two groups.

2. Have one child pick a card and read it to his or her group.

3. Have children raise their hands to answer the questions.

4. When a child gets the answer right, give him or her a clue to where an item of clothing is hidden in the room. When the child finds it, he or she can put the clothing item on the body for his or her team.

5. The team that dresses their body first wins.

Make a Book or PSA Poster

Purpose: In this activity, we will work out an easy-to-follow process for children to use to get help if their body space is invaded.

Materials: Posters, art materials

Preparation:

1. Have children discuss what it means when someone invades their body privacy and what they need to do if that happens. Use leading questions to help them come to steps that are similar to the following:

   a. Tell them, "Don't touch me."
   b. Call for help.
   c. Tell an adult what happened.

2. Have children make a list of things they would say to other kids to let them know that people should not invade their body privacy.

Procedure:

1. Split the children into groups of two or three.

2. Have each group make a poster to hang in the halls that will help their friends to know what to do if someone invades their body privacy.

Friendship Cards—Appropriate Body

Purpose: The friendship cards are used as a visual reminder for the children, to reinforce the concept that has been taught.

Materials: The following friendship cards found in Appendix A:

- Things We Do to Respect Our Friends' Body Privacy
- What I Do if Someone Invades My Body Privacy

Preparation: See directions in "How to Use This Book."

Procedure: See directions in "How to Use This Book."

Generalization and Consistency

- When children accidentally touch someone inappropriately, refer them to the friendship cards of appropriate touch.
- Treat this lesson as a teaching opportunity and avoid judgmental attitudes.

LESSON 5: MODESTY/HYGIENE

Introduction/Overview

We define modesty as the appropriate way we outwardly portray our bodies in the way we dress. We have paired modesty with hygiene in this chapter to help children develop an outward image that attracts others to them. We live in a very visual society, and the way someone looks affects others' impression. Many children who have difficulty with social interaction do not have a firm grasp on proper hygiene and dress. In this lesson, we will look at modesty and hygiene and how we dress and take care of our bodies.

Teaching Concepts

- Keeping ourselves clean and healthy helps us to be happy and have fun.
- Staying clean and healthy helps us to make and keep friends.
- Keeping our bodies clean, healthy, and dressed makes it easier for others to be our friend.

Attitude

- Accept that children have trouble grasping certain safety concepts.
- We want to avoid having children feel shame. We can be private about our bodies without feeling ashamed of them.

Lesson Objective

- Children will identify what habits are needed every day to keep proper hygiene.
- Children will identify why proper hygiene is important.
- Children will list why proper hygiene helps them to make and keep friends.

Lesson Introduction

Brainstorm for Key Concepts

Have children develop lists to refer to by asking specific questions. Use the directions found in the "How to use this book" section. Here are some suggestions for questions to ask:

- What do we do in the morning to be neat and clean?
- What do we do during the day to be neat and clean?
- What do we do at night to be neat and clean?
- How does keeping neat and clean help us to make and keep friends?

Activities

Washing of the Germs Game

Purpose: To help children get a real sense of how difficult it is to keep their hands clean and how thoroughly they need to wash.

Materials: Glitter (green and purple are best), water, soap, sinks/water tubs, paper towels, drop cloth, "Washing Our Hands" chart (see Appendix B).

Preparation: Make sure there are enough paper towels for all children; lay drop cloths over the area where the activity will be done.

Procedure:

1. Review the concept development that was done in the introduction to this lesson about how it is important to keep ourselves clean.

2. Show the glitter to the children and let them know that you are pretending the glitter specks are germs for the day.

3. Using the "Washing Our Hands" chart, practice (without water) the proper way to wash hands.

4. Have each child come and put a hand in the "germ" mix and get germs on his or her hands. Then have the children use the water in the tubs to wash off the glitter germs.

5. Point out how hard they need to work to get their hands clean.

Dress the Best Game

Purpose: The purpose of this game is to have the children look at the different ways people can get dressed in a fun and silly way. It gives children the opportunity to look critically at someone's attire without attacking anyone's self-esteem.

Materials: A paper doll for each child

Preparation: None

Procedure:

1. Split the children into groups of two to four.

2. Have the children color in the paper dolls. Ask half the children in each group to color in a well-dressed doll based on the brainstorming, and ask the other half to color in a messy doll.

3. After the pictures are colored, have the children cut their dolls into three parts and put all the parts into three piles according to top, bottom, and middle. Shuffle each pile.

4. Each child is to pick one body part from each pile and put the person puzzle together. Then, have each child say which part of the body is best dressed and tell what the person should change about the other parts.

5. For small groups or one-on-ones, make a best-dressed flip book with funny people and discuss the parts that are best dressed and what should be changed.

Make a Book to Teach Others About a Topic

Purpose: The purpose of this activity is to bring together the concepts in this lesson.

Materials: Paper, markers

Preparation: Review the posters and brainstorm concepts the children have created so far.

Procedure:

1. Have the children make a book about privacy with one page for each concept from brainstorming.

2. Have children share their books with the class. When children are having difficulty respecting body privacy, review the books and help them pick more appropriate behaviors.

3. For younger groups, work together to make one book, with each child being responsible for one page.

Friendship Cards—Appropriate Body

Purpose: The friendship cards are used as a visual reminder for the children, to reinforce the concept that has been taught.

Materials: The following friendship cards found in Appendix A:

- What We Do in the Morning to Be Neat and Clean
- What We Do During the Day to Be Neat and Clean
- What We Do at Night to Be Neat and Clean

Preparation: See directions in "How to Use This Book."

Procedure: See directions in "How to Use This Book."

Generalization and Consistency

- Hang PSA posters.
- Use a daily chart and give out stars for cleanliness with prizes at the end of each week.
- Have children self-evaluate hygiene and modesty by giving themselves three to five stars on a list of 8 to 10 things they do the best and one to two checks on things they would like to improve. Revisit the chart in 2 to 3 weeks.

LESSON 6: APPROPRIATE BODIES IN DIFFERENT ENVIRONMENTS

Introduction/Overview

Some children also have difficulty regulating their sensory systems. That is, they will get overstimulated in situations where there are many sights and sounds to deal with and act inappropriately as a result. We suggest consulting with an occupational therapist (OT) who has Sensory Integration Training when you are dealing with children who have difficulty moving at the right speed in social settings. In this lesson, we will be helping children identify when and why we move our bodies at different speeds in different places. Many children have not been taught how to observe an environment and assess the way their body speed affects their social interactions. The goal is to show each child that there are appropriate times and places for different body speeds and how to choose the appropriate one for the situation.

Teaching Concepts

- Everyone has different sensory needs.
- There is an appropriate body speed for every situation.

Attitude

- All body speeds are good (even fast body).
- Everyone has different sensory solutions.
- We need to give children the time they need to process their own sensory input.

Lesson Objective

- Children will identify what body speeds are appropriate in different social settings.
- Children will accept suggestion to help change their body speed.
- Children will identify the different body speeds.

Lesson Introduction

Brainstorm for Key Concepts

Have children develop lists to refer to by asking them specific questions. Use the directions found in the "How to Use This Book" section.

Using place cards in Appendix B, have children make a brainstorming list of how they should act in the different environments. Put their ideas in categories of fast, focused, or slow. Then ask the children to write their answers to the following questions:

- What happens if we move fast in a slow place, such as a Library?
- What happens if we move too slowly in a fast place like when we are playing a sport?
- What helps us to speed up?
- What helps to slow down?
- Why should we try to change the speed our body is going?

Activities

Freeze Dance With Various Music Speeds

Purpose: Using music, this activity helps children experience and differentiate among various activities and body speeds.

Materials: CD player, CDs with music at different speeds (suggestion: have one rock CD, one classical/lullaby CD, and one kid CD at medium speed)

Preparation: None

Procedure:

1. Have children each find a place in the room to stand.

2. Tell the children that you want them to guess which body speed they should use to move and dance to the music. Tell them that when the music stops, they should freeze.

3. Play a piece of music and have the children yell out the body speed they think it is. It will be difficult for children to distinguish between focused and fast. Play the two examples repeatedly to help them become accustomed to each.

4. Have the children dance to the beat of the music and demonstrate the different levels of movement. Help the children understand to slow down for slow body-speed music, speed up for the fast body-speed music, and find the balance between the two for focused body-speed music.

Polaroid of Each Body Speed

Purpose: This activity helps children review the different body speeds and gives them the opportunity to act out each level.

Materials: Polaroid camera, film to take two to three pictures of each child, glue

Preparation: None

Procedure:

1. Either during or after the Freeze Dance activity, take pictures of the children moving and acting out each level.

2. Have each child tell you which level he or she was acting out in each picture.

Brainstorm Words to Match Speeds

Purpose: To give children a greater understanding of body speeds and their meaning. This activity is good for visual learners who enjoy reading and words.

Materials: Lists of locations and how we act from the Lesson Introduction (new list or one that has already been created), paper, and markers

Preparation: None

Procedure:

1. Have the children brainstorm different words that can represent the body speeds, such as the following:

   a. Colors (fast = red, orange; slow = blue, purple)
   b. Temperatures (fast = hot; slow = cool)
   c. Adjectives (fast = wild, excited; slow = sleepy)

2. Have each child pick a word from the list and write it in bubble letters and decorate it.

Game of Matching Pictures to Speed

Purpose: This activity reinforces the concept of appropriate body speeds and gives children the opportunity to observe various body speeds in others.

Materials: Place cards, Polaroid pictures of the different body speeds

Preparation: Make two piles, one of the photos of the children and one of the places cards.

Procedure:

1. Divide children into teams and have them go through and match the pictures with the appropriate location.

2. Have children discuss the different locations and why they matched the pictures that they did.

Don't Break the Ice by Milton Bradley

Purpose: This is a great game to help children who have trouble controlling their impulses. In order to be successful in the game, children need to control the rate and strength of tapping. This is a challenge for some children, and this game is a fun way to help them work on it.

Materials: The Don't Break the Ice game

Preparation: See game directions.

Procedure:

1. Have a discussion with the children about how the game is played and how they need to use gentle banging.

2. Set up the game as described in the directions and allow the children to bang the ice cubes as hard as they want for a test and to let them get it out of their system.

3. Play the game as explained in the directions.

Pete's a Pizza

Purpose: In this activity, the children will see a child doing sensory input games with his family.

Materials: The book *Pete's a Pizza* by William Steig, paper plates, construction paper, crayons

Preparation: Cut out red circles for pepperoni. Cut construction paper into small pieces to be cheese or use leftovers from paper shredder.

Procedure:

1. Read the book *Pete's a Pizza,* by William Steig, aloud to the children.

2. Have the children guess how Pete's body felt *before* his father made him into a pizza.

3. Have the children guess how Pete felt *after* his dad made him into a pizza.

4. Have a sensory experience with the children by acting out the book. Have adults go from child to child to turn the children into pizzas or have children pair off and turn each other into pizzas.

5. Do an art project where children make pizzas out of paper plates. Have children color and cut out the pizza toppings, use markers to color the paper plate with "pizza sauce," and glue the topping on.

6. Another option is to allow the children to make pizzas out of play dough.

Musical Islands

Purpose: In musical islands, children play like musical chairs, but they are asked to share spots as some are taken away. The object of the game is to have all the children sharing one spot at the end without anyone getting knocked down. This game helps children go from a fast-moving pace to moving carefully so that no one gets knocked over. This activity can be used with many of the lessons, and it can also be used as sensory filler just to give the children move-around time.

Materials: Polyspots or construction paper taped to the ground, CD player and music CDs

Preparation: Lay spots out on the ground spaced one to two feet apart.

Procedure:

1. Have children find a spot of their own to stand on. Explain the rules of the game and point out that all they need is to be *touching* the spot to be considered "on the island." Remind the children that they need to move their bodies at a speed that will keep their friends safe and no one will get knocked over.

2. When the music starts, have the children get off the spots and dance around the room.

3. When the music stops, the children must each pick a new spot to stand on.

4. After two or three stops in the music, start by taking one or two spots away from the children when the music stops.

5. The children need to share spots. Even having one toe on the spot counts.

6. Play until all the children are sharing one spot.

Silly Speed Pictures

Purpose: We use this activity to help the children begin to brainstorm the different things that they should use their various body speeds for.

Materials: Paper and art supplies, poster, place cards

Preparation: None

Procedure:

1. Brainstorm with children what is good to do when they are at the different speeds.

2. Draw pictures of activities/experiences of each level. Draw pictures of different body speeds.

3. Have children take turns picking cards from a pile. Have children identify what speed is needed in the place they chose.

4. Have children guess what would happen if they used the wrong speed in the environments (example: Using a fast speed in a library). Draw pictures of the different silly speeds.

Friendship Cards—Appropriate Body

Purpose: The friendship cards are used as a visual reminder for the children, to reinforce the concept that has been taught.

Materials: The following friendship cards found in Appendix A:

- How We Slow Our Body When It Is Too Fast
- How We Get Our Body Moving When It Is Too Slow
- Places for Fast Body Speed
- Places for Slow Body Speed
- Places for Listening Body

Preparation: See directions in "How to Use This Book."

Procedure: See directions in "How to Use This Book."

Generalization and Consistency

- Let children know what speed their bodies should be moving in different social settings.
- Refer children to friendship cards for suggestions for changing body speeds.
- Offer sensory input (such as jumping in place, spinning, or clapping hands) to children before and after times of focus to help the children attend to what is going on.

UNIT 5

Interacting in a Group

The skills that support positive abilities to work in a group include incorporating the concepts taught in the previous lessons. Those basic concepts give the children the foundation to interact in a group in a variety of environments. This unit was developed to take the previously learned skills and continue to generalize them into a group setting. This unit will not only teach the skills necessary to work in this group setting, but it will also allow each child the opportunity to use the strategies learned to interact in a variety of environments.

Social Goals

- Children will stay on topic when contributing to a group discussion in a classroom setting.
- Children will use positive language to share ideas and make suggestions on group projects.
- Children will use skills such as organizing others, giving directions, listening to ideas, and encouraging participation when interacting in a group.
- Children will choose (unprompted/unfacilitated) to complete a game with a group.
- Children will respect personal space of peers and adults during a group activity.
- Children will use the skills taught to maintain focus and attention in a group environment.
- Children will use appropriate levels of movement and energy for different activities and environments.
- Children will use visual supports to increase participation in and contributions to a group project.

LESSON 1: LISTENING IN A GROUP

Introduction/Overview

The listening skills learned in Unit 2, "Making Eye Contact for Interaction," although they may have been taught in a group setting, focused on the eye contact skills needed for listening during one-to-one interactions. This lesson will develop the listening skills necessary to maintain interaction in a group environment or with the leader of a group. Teaching strategies for listening increases the children's ability to focus and attend to in-group settings. Listening in a group setting increases the challenge of attending for children who have auditory sensitivities. The extra noise, visual activity, and possible larger space add to the challenge of listening to retain information or show others that the child is listening. Once again, eye contact is both the cue to others that the child is listening and is critical in assisting in a child's ability to attend.

Teaching Concepts

- Listening to the leader of the group helps children to follow along with the group.
- Listening to the other members of the group helps children to be a part of the group.
- Listening is the best way for children to show everyone in the group that they are involved in the activity.
- Looking at others helps children to listen.

Attitude

- Children with attention/focus challenges have an even harder time listening in a group.
- Some children may need additional visual supports (such as lists of directions) to help them follow along in a group activity.
- The louder the environment, the harder it is to listen.

Lesson Objective

- Children will increase their ability to participate in a group by learning how to listen in a group.
- Children will learn to ask for help when needed when they are not able to listen or attend.
- Children will learn how to listen to others' ideas and show respect for an idea even though they may not agree with it.
- Children will develop the ability to listen to others so they will know when to contribute to a conversation.

Lesson Introduction

Concept Map—"Listening in a Group"

Have the children help develop a concept map by asking them leading questions. Use the directions found in the "How to Use This Book" section.

When teaching the concepts on the map, try first acting out the wrong way to listen in a group, to add humor to the children's learning. Then ask the children to help model the right way to listen and look interested.

Figure 5.1   Concept Map: Listening in a Group

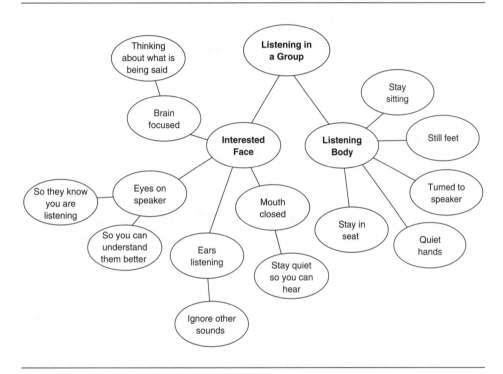

Activities

Gross Motor Group Cooperative Activities—Parachute Keep Up, Skis, Tug-of-War

Purpose: To help the children learn that they need to listen to others to be able to participate. The Stride-R ski by Sportime is perfect for pairs of children to practice working together as a team and to learn listening skills. The Preparation and Procedure sections below include directions for using the skis. If you choose another of the gross motor cooperative activities listed above, just adapt the directions accordingly. The intention behind the activity should remain the same.

Materials: Stride-R skis, parachute, or rope (depending on the activity you choose)

Preparation: Draw or use tape to make a start and a finish line.

Procedure:

1. Divide children into pairs.

2. Demonstrate how to use the skis.

3. Have children choose who will be in front and who will be in back in each pair (you may want to refer to the "Who Goes First?" section in Unit 6, "Playing Games").

4. Run the race.

5. Afterward, talk about what helped and what didn't when racing.

6. Run the race again, reminding the children of the things they said helped or did not help them in the race.

Noisy Whisper Down the Lane

Purpose: To increase children's listening skills to better attend in a group by providing an additional challenge of background noise.

Materials: None

Preparation: Make a list of directions that will be used in a group project. Gauge the complexity of the directions based on the age and skill level of the group.

Procedure:

1. Have children sit on the floor or in chairs next to each other in rows of four or five.

2. Explain the rules to "Noisy Whisper Down the Lane" (see below).

3. Whisper the first direction to the first child in each row.

4. Either have the last child write the direction down or have the child tell it to an adult for him or her to write it down.

5. When the direction is written, start again with the second direction until all the directions are given.

6. Have each row read their list aloud and see how close they are to the real list.

7. Repeat the same activity adding music or some other background noise.

8. Compare both lists and discuss the challenges of listening when there is extra noise.

9. Discuss the importance of listening to follow directions. Use the best list to make a project.

Brainstorming for a Topic

Purpose: To illustrate the importance of listening to each other in a group.

Materials: Paper, pencil, idea for project

Preparation: Make copies of the "Brainstorm for a Group Project" worksheet in Appendix B, enough for each group to have one.

Procedure:

1. Decide on a project for the children. Examples: puppet show, party, or play

2. Break the children into groups of 3–5. Have them move their groups to different areas in the room.

3. Describe the theme for the project.

4. Hand out the brainstorm sheets to each group.

5. Assign one child in each group to write down all the ideas as well as the group's final choice.

6. Let them go and observe their listening abilities while they brainstorm. Try to facilitate as little as possible. Redirect the children back to the group whenever possible.

7. Give them a countdown to finish.

8. Bring them back and ask them what they came up with. Questions to ask might include the following:

   a. Did everyone in your group agree on a topic?
   b. What were some of the ideas?
   c. Who had trouble listening to the others? Why?
   d. Who didn't get heard? Why?

9. As a group, develop a list of ways to help everyone listen when brainstorming ideas (refer back to original concept map).

10. Use this list and idea for future group projects.

Friendship Cards—Interacting in a Group

Purpose: The friendship cards are used as a visual reminder for the children, to reinforce the concept that has been taught.

Materials: The following friendship cards found in Appendix A:

- Interested Face
- Listening Body

Preparation: See directions in "How to Use This Book."

Procedure: See directions in "How to Use This Book."

Generalization and Consistency

- Directly requesting eye contact is the most successful method for strengthening children's eye contact when they are listening and talking.
- Ask for eye contact when the children are making statements or requesting objects.
- Put the emphasis on the fact that only when they use eye contact does the other person know they are listening or speaking to him or her.
- Give positive feedback to the children when they show great listening skills by following directions or answering questions with appropriate answers.
- If the children are not successful in a game or activity, brainstorm ways for them to increase their listening skills so as to improve their chances of success.

LESSON 2: SOCIALIZING IN A GROUP

Introduction/Overview

To interact and work successfully in a group, a person needs to strengthen his or her ability to multitask. The skills that are used when multitasking are listening, focusing on the activity, positively interacting, and initiating interactions with others. The activities chosen for this lesson are dramatic play scenarios or group projects. If the children know and use the skills needed to be able to play with others in dramatic play settings, they will be more successful in other group activities. It may be necessary to start with a dramatic play scenario for younger children or use a group project for older children, but look for positive interaction skills in either situation. It may be helpful to refer to the "Being a Friend" unit (Unit 3) and the lessons that teach sweet/kind words to support positive interaction skills during group interactions.

Teaching Concepts

- Interacting with the group helps to make the activity fun.
- Being a part of a group activity requires many tasks, and learning the tasks makes being with others easier and more fun.
- Teaching group skills can be accomplished while children are playing with others in a group activity.

Attitude

- Children can be more successful in group activities if taught the individual skills needed to play and interact in a group.

- Learning how to play in a group helps younger children learn the basic skills that will be necessary to work in groups when they are older.
- Sensitivity to all the skills needed and understanding that these skills can be taught and learned help to increase a child's success in interacting.

Lesson Objective

- Children will learn positive communication skills necessary to interact with others in a group.
- Children will learn to initiate interactions and get someone's attention in a group environment.
- Children will increase their ability to focus attention on other members of the group.

Lesson Introduction

Brainstorm for Key Concepts

Have children develop lists to refer to by asking them specific questions. Use the directions found in the "How to Use This Book" section. Here are some suggestions for questions to ask:

- What are the types of words we use when talking to our friends? List the sweet/kind words we have learned before when we talk to our friends.
- What are the words or phrases we can use to share ideas with our friends?
- How do we get people's attention when we want to talk to them?
- What can you do to help you pay more attention to others when talking to them in a group?

Activities

Dramatic Play Center

Purpose: This group activity gives children the chance to interact with peers, use their imagination, use positive language, share, take turns, and initiate basic problem-solving ideas. It is also a great opportunity to observe the children's dramatic play skills and learn both their interaction strengths and challenges. This is the first activity to build group skills. Modify the toys or theme to fit the children's interest and age.

Materials: Dolls or toy figures; theme-based play scenario such as farm with animals, dollhouse, or castle with knights and princesses. Also have available additional toys such as blocks to offer for children to expand the play theme.

Preparation: Arrange a center area with enough space for the children to move around comfortably but one that is blocked off so children won't wander away from the interaction. Have toys organized on shelves or in baskets so children can easily get to them and see what is available.

Procedure:

1. Introduce the play theme to the children.

2. Show the children all the toys available.

3. Make sure there are enough toys for each child to easily participate.

4. Observe the children's play and facilitate as needed. Make suggestions to children to expand the play scenario. Prompt positive language and mediate any conflicts. Allow the children enough time to self-correct but then step in when needed.

Group Project

Purpose: This is the next step in helping children to successfully work in a group. Use the ideas the children decided on using the worksheets in the Listening in a Group lesson. This is a multistep activity that may take a few sessions. It is beneficial to check in with children (individually if necessary) to note their participation and understanding. Tell the children that each of them should have at least one task on the to-do list.

Materials: "Brainstorm for a Group Project" worksheets from Listening in a Group lesson; "Group Project To-Do List" and "Group Meeting Notes" worksheets found in Appendix B.

Preparation: Make copies of the "Group Project To-Do List" and "Group Meeting Notes" worksheets for each group.

Procedure:

1. Have children get back into their brainstorming groups from the "Listening in a Group" lesson.

2. Have the children use the topic they decided on to begin planning the group project.

3. Explain how to use the "Group Project To-Do List" and "Group Meeting Notes" worksheets.

4. Allow the children as much independence as possible while planning their group project.

5. Check-ins with the children are extremely important, especially if you see any struggles or conflicts.

6. Check in with the group as a whole at the end of each session to ask for feedback about the group's progress. Use the worksheets the children have filled out to ask specific questions about the project. The more specific the questions, the more likely it will be that you will get responses about the children's actual progress.

Friendship Cards—Interacting in a Group

Purpose: The friendship cards are used as a visual reminder for the children, to reinforce the concept that has been taught.

Materials: The following friendship cards found in Appendix A:

- Words to Use When Sharing Ideas
- Ways to Get Someone's Attention

Preparation: See directions in "How to Use This Book."

Procedure: See directions in "How to Use This Book."

Generalization and Consistency

- When a child is interrupting others in a group setting, ask the child to wait until the present conversation is finished and then he or she will have an opportunity to speak. Remind the child frequently that what he or she has to say is important and to please wait until it is his or her turn.
- When a child raises his or her hand during instructions or directions, ask the child if it is a question, comment, or story. If it is a question, ask the child to wait until you have given all the directions. If it is a comment or story, tell the child to wait until the lesson or project begins, and then you will listen to him or her.
- When asking the children to contribute to a group discussion or when giving verbal directions, request their eye contact; state the question or direction slowly, giving them specific cues, then wait for them to respond.
- Creating more opportunity for children to have leadership roles and interactions in which they need to be invested will help them develop a comfort in being involved.
- Have children take on major roles in an activity such as a particular responsibility or decision-making role in order to strengthen their confidence.

LESSON 3: LEARNING IN A GROUP

Introduction/Overview

The aspects of learning in a group correspond to the concepts of interacting in a group. The added challenge for children is the learning of new information that requires increased attention and focusing skills. Additional supports are often needed to meet a child's specific challenges. Use of visual supports or physical movement often increases a child's ability to learn. Also, many children have the ability to appear as if they are attending when they are not. Checking in is a necessity to make sure a child is retaining the information given. Practicing by using additional supports and strategies will increase a child's ability to retain information in the future.

Teaching Concepts

- It is as much fun to learn with others as it is to learn on our own.
- Remind children that if they get confused or are not sure of what to do, they can ask for help.
- Written directions can help children follow along with the group activity.

Attitude

- Learning in a group environment has many possible additional challenges.
- Children can benefit from increased visual support and more specific instructions to increase their ability to be successful in a group project.
- If a child is having trouble contributing to the group activity, adapting the activity for the child should always be done first, before behavior modification is attempted.

Lesson Objective

- Children will learn skills to increase their attention to the activity.
- Children will learn to utilize visual supports offered to help them participate in the group activity.
- Children will increase their awareness of how to use their body appropriately in a group of friends.

Lesson Introduction

Concept Map—"What Helps Us Learn in a Group?"

Have the children help develop a concept map by asking them leading questions. Use the directions found in the "How to Use This Book" section.

Activities

Clue Hunt

Purpose: This is a small-group activity that allows the children to work together to find the answer with the clues that are hidden. The skills that should be reinforced include listening, using eye contact, positive language, focusing, impulse control, and body space awareness.

Materials: Clue cards found in Appendix B

Figure 5.2   Concept Map: What Helps Us Learn in a Group?

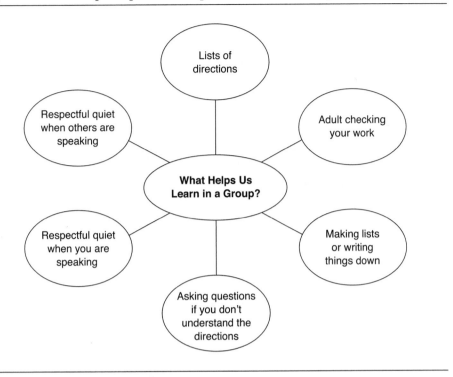

Preparation: Photocopy clue cards and cut them out. Color clue cards if you think the additional visual support would increase the focusing ability of the children in your group.

Procedure:

1. Hide the three clues around the room. Have only 3 to 5 children per group. Two or more groups can be hunting for clues at the same time. Make sure the groups are separated enough so the children do not find each other's clues.

2. Explain that this is a group game, so the whole group must try to figure out the answer.

3. Once all three clues are found, have the children bring them to a table or specific area to begin thinking as a group about the answer.

4. The group needs to check with each member to agree on an answer before the group tells the facilitator.

5. Once they figure out the answer, group members raise their hands to tell the facilitator the answer.

6. If they are correct, you can have the group hide their eyes so you can hide more clues.

7. If the group answers incorrectly, tell them to try to think as a group again for the answer.

Goop Project

Purpose: This group activity can be adapted to use any simple recipe. We chose goop because the end result gives sensory input and feels really cool. Keep in mind that the tactile feeling of the goop may be too challenging for some children. The focus of this activity is to use a simple recipe and allow a small group of children to work together to make something.

Materials: A copy of the goop recipe for each group of children (pictures can be added to the written directions for beginning readers to increase independence), ingredients listed in the recipe, measuring utensils, mixing bowls, spoons, individual containers

Preparation: Adapt recipe if necessary. Make copies of recipe for each group. Assemble supplies and utensils.

Procedure:

1. Assemble children into small groups.

2. Explain activity. Read recipe aloud and use the supplies as visual support when describing the activity.

3. Have children make the goop. Try to allow as much independence as possible.

4. When the children have finished, allow them time to explore the goop either as a group or pour it into individual containers.

Swimmy *Book Project*

Purpose: This activity combines using a story that teaches positive friendship skills with a group activity to help generalize the group skills taught in the Lesson Introduction.

Materials: Swimmy by Leo Lionni, large roll of paper, small paper plates, scissors, stapler, red and blue paint, glue

Preparation: Assemble supplies. Draw large fish outline on poster. Make little fish by cutting out a small triangle at the edge of each plate for the mouth and stapling this to the other side of the plate to make the tail.

Procedure:

1. Read book to children.

2. Have children paint the poster blue around the fish.

3. Have children paint all but one of the little paper-plate fish red.

4. Paint one of the paper-plate fishes black.

5. Glue small red fish onto poster inside the outline of the big fish. Fill this whole area with red fish.

6. Use the black fish in the space where the eye of the big fish should be.

7. When finished, review with the children the friendship skills that are used by the fish in the story.

Friendship Cards—Interacting in a Group

Purpose: The friendship cards are used as a visual reminder for the children, to reinforce the concept that has been taught.

Materials: The following friendship card found in Appendix A:

- Ways We Learn in a Group

Preparation: See directions in "How to Use This Book."

Procedure: See directions in "How to Use This Book."

Generalization and Consistency

- When a child gets distracted, help with recall and developing focus by restating the directions instead of telling the child to stop what he or she is doing.
- Use redirecting phrases such as "Remember the directions," "What should you be doing now?" or "What did I say were the directions?"
- If a child or children benefit from the visual supports used, generalize this strategy in other environments to help the children attend and focus better.

LESSON 4: ADULT-LED GROUPS

Introduction/Overview

In classroom settings, all children will get some experience in an adult-led group. The objective of this is to develop their ability to attend in a meaningful way to the interactive nuances. Without proper instruction in the skills needed to attend in groups, children can easily get lost in the flow of the interaction. This sense of confusion can frustrate a child and often lead to inappropriate behaviors in group settings. With proper instruction and practice, children are able to be productive members of groups and have rich learning experiences.

Teaching Concepts

- We learn from the information we gather from groups.
- Group settings are good environments for us to share our ideas.
- We learn from others.

Attitude

- The length of the circle time/meeting time should be based on the children's attention span, not our lesson plan.
- Sensory input is a necessity for all children in order for them to be successful.
- Integration of visual, verbal, experiential, repetitious, and kinesthetic learning should be embedded in all circle and meeting times.

Lesson Objective

- Children will strengthen their ability to attend for extended durations.
- Children will follow teaching themes in a group setting.
- Children will raise hands, take turns, and participate appropriately in a group setting.

Lesson Introduction

Concept Map—"Circle Time/Meeting Time"

Have the children help develop a concept map by asking them leading questions. Use the directions found in the "How to Use This Book" section.

Figure 5.3   Concept Map: Circle Time/Meeting Time

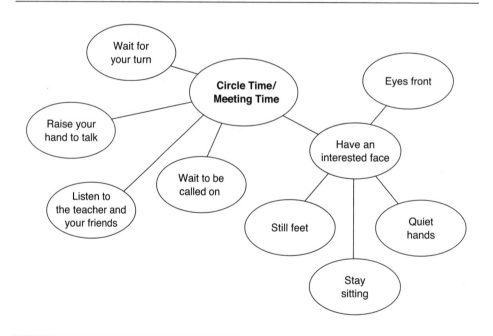

Activities

Draw an Interested Face

Purpose: This activity will build awareness in the children not only of how to increase their attention and listening but also how to look more interested while attending.

Materials: Hand mirror for each child or one larger mirror for the group, markers, crayons, "Interested Face" outlines found in Appendix B.

Preparation: Make copies of face outlines, one for each child, and assemble supplies.

Procedure:

1. While children are looking in the mirror, have them practice making interested faces.

2. Split the children into pairs and have one child draw the other child making an interested face.

3. When they are finished, have them switch so the other child has the opportunity to draw.

4. Have children share the pictures with the group when finished.

I Am Going on a Picnic

Purpose: To have children follow a play theme and attend to conversation in a group setting.

Materials: Use a ball or other visual cue to help children understand whose turn it is.

Preparation: None

Procedure:

1. The adult goes first and says, "I am going on a picnic and I am going to bring apples" (or something else that begins with the letter A).

2. The next person says the same thing, adding something with the letter B. ("I am going on a picnic and I am going to bring apples and bananas.")

3. Continue the game until someone can't remember an item. That child gets to start the next round.

4. We suggest that no one is considered "out" in this game. Continue to give the children the opportunity to attend.

Outburst Jr. (by Parker Brothers)

Purpose: To strengthen children's focus and control in an exciting activity.

Materials: Outburst Jr. game by Parker Brothers

Preparation: None

Procedure:

1. Play game according to the instructions. Have children raise their hand in order to guess.

2. Alternate between allowing children to yell out answers for one round and raise their hand for the next.

3. Discuss the pros and cons of playing each of these ways.

Friendship Cards—Interacting in a Group

Purpose: The friendship cards are used as a visual reminder for the children, to reinforce the concept that has been taught.

Materials: The following friendship card found in Appendix A:

- Circle Time/Meeting Time

Preparation: See directions in "How to Use This Book."

Procedure: See directions in "How to Use This Book."

Generalization and Consistency

- When a child raises his or her hand during instructions or directions, ask the child if it is a question, comment, or story. If it is a question, ask the child to wait until you have given all the directions. If it is a comment or story, tell the child to wait until the lesson or project begins, and then you will listen to him or her.
- Offer adult-directed opportunities where the children are redirected back to the activity and reassure them of when it will be their turn.

UNIT 6

Playing Games

Introduction/Overview

In this unit, we will be working on appropriate play in a variety of settings. So many of the children we work with have difficulty in play situations due to the lack of knowledge of how to play. In this lesson, we are helping the children develop play vocabulary and practice the skills needed for interactive play.

Social Goals

- Children will use appropriate language and attitude when playing.
- Children will identify what sportsmanship is and use it in a play setting.
- Children will be able to suggest and use a fair method of figuring out who goes first.
- Children will play indoor games by following the rules and using positive interaction skills.
- Children will be able to identify and exercise safety during outdoor play.
- Children will be able to play video games interactively with others in different environments.

LESSON 1: SPORTSMANSHIP/CHEERING AND ENCOURAGEMENT

Introduction/Overview

We often see conflict between children in a play situation when they are using negative language and attitudes toward each other. Almost always, this happens when one child is not doing things the way his or her friends want. Most children have been exposed to so much negative response to these types of situations that it is the only way they know to react to their frustration. This is where the conflict happens. Instead of using positive language to support others, they use critical, aggressive tones. In this lesson, we will teach children how to encourage each other during play and to use positive sportsmanship at the end of games.

Teaching Concepts

- We cheer for our friends to show that we like them.
- We give encouragement before, during, and after playing.
- Cheering helps us as well as the others who are playing.
- We are supportive with friends who win as well as friends who lose.
- We encourage others when we win.
- We play positively or we don't play.

Attitude

- Adults need to exaggerate our cheering to help children see how big it should be.
- It is difficult to see past losing to encourage the win, and this might take some time.
- There is no reason to feel bad about not winning.

Lesson Objective

- Children will identify the different ways to cheer their friends.
- Children will list the times and places to encourage others.
- Children will list the benefits of being supportive of friends.
- Children will practice cheering for each other in a game.

Lesson Introduction

Brainstorm for Key Concepts

Have children develop lists to refer to by asking them specific questions. Use the directions found in the "How to Use This Book" section.

- Ask the children to define sportsmanship or being a good sport.
- Have children list ways to encourage/cheer others.
- Brainstorm when we should use these cheers.
- Have children list different places to encourage/cheer.
- Ask children why we encourage/cheer others.

Activities

Copy the Design/Best the Time

Purpose: In this game, the children are asked to work as a group under a time pressure. In a situation like this, non-sportsmanlike language usually is used out of frustration.

Materials: "Copy the Picture" worksheet (see Appendix B), markers

Preparation: Copy worksheet so there is enough for each child to have two or three.

Procedure:

1. Separate children into two teams or into pairs.

2. Give each child a paper with a silly design on it.

3. Give each team/pair one marker to share.

4. Tell the children they will need to work quickly so that everyone can copy their designs before the timer goes off.

5. When the timer starts, the children must quickly copy or trace the silly designs. When they are done, they pass the marker to their partner or to the next person in the group.

6. Encourage the children to use the cheers they had brainstormed to help their friends.

7. Try the game again with everyone being silent.

8. Discuss with the children which way they liked better. Find out which was more fun. Point out the time it took to finish the design.

Friend Fan Poster

Purpose: In this activity, children will create a poster that is in support of a friend.

Materials: Poster or large paper for each child, markers and art supplies

Preparation: Start activity by having children brainstorm what things they would put on a poster to cheer on a local sports hero if they were going to see the person play.

Procedure:

1. Have children pair off. (As an extra challenge for older groups, pick children's names out of a hat to make pairs so that they are making posters for people with whom they spend less time.) Make sure to prompt the children about "sweet words" and positive language and tell them that the goal is to encourage a friend.

2. Have each child share something that he or she likes about the friend the child is paired with or why the friend is a good sport. (If children are picking names out of a hat, use this as an open question time in which children can ask their partner questions to get to know what game they like to play and what strengths to cheer for.)

3. Ask children to pretend that the friend is involved in a sports game and that they are going to cheer for that friend.

4. Using markers and poster board, have each child make a poster to cheer for that friend.

5. Have each child share the poster that he or she made about the friend.

Obstacle Course/Beat the Time

Purpose: This is a gross motor game that will challenge the children to use positive sportsmanship. Here there is the pressure of a time constraint that will test the children's ability to stay calm and not use negative language with peers who are slower or more challenged.

Materials: Gross motor equipment or furniture

Preparation: Set up an obstacle course in a safe space.

Procedure:

1. This activity can be done as a large group or by splitting the class into teams of two.

2. Have the group(s) go through the obstacle course and time how long it takes for all of the students to complete the course.

3. Go through the course again, and this time, have the children cheer for each member of the group as they go through.

4. Compare times and discuss how it felt when others were cheering for them. Point out if any children were using negative comments, and ask children to discuss if that is effective in supporting a teammate.

5. Game modification: If space is limited or children are too old for obstacle courses, use the same procedure for a relay race. Races such as balancing a cotton ball on a spoon, holding a balloon under the chin, or running with a playground ball between the knees are challenging and add a silly aspect to keep things fun.

Friendship Cards—Playing Games

Purpose: The friendship cards are used as a visual reminder for the children, to reinforce the concept that has been taught.

Materials: The following friendship cards found in Appendix A:

- A Good Sport
- Ways to Cheer Your Friends

Preparation: See directions in "How to Use This Book."

Procedure: See directions in "How to Use This Book."

Generalization and Consistency

- Hang brainstorming list and encouragement posters in the classroom and refer to them before competitive activities or if the children forget to use positive encouragement.

LESSON 2: WHO GOES FIRST?

Introduction/Overview

Over the years, we have been surprised at how often we come across children who have no idea how to figure out a fair way to determine who will go first. It amazes us how many times children will go back and forth saying "I want to go first" not realizing that this does not create a solution for them. In this lesson, we will introduce ways of figuring out who goes first and explore the importance of not always going first.

Teaching Concepts

- Figuring out who goes first is something we must do fairly.
- Going first is not always important.
- We do not have to go first to win. We can also win if we go second, third, or fourth.

Attitude

- The thrill of going first is very enticing and very difficult to let go of.
- Many children have not been taught how to figure out who goes first.

Lesson Objective

- Children will identify different fair ways to figure out who goes first.
- Children will have the experience of trying a new way of determining who goes first.
- Children will calmly accept others going first.

Lesson Introduction

Brainstorm for Key Concepts

Have children develop lists to refer to by asking them specific questions. Use the directions found in the "How to Use This Book" section. If children have challenges thinking of ways to figure out who goes first, here are some ideas to help them:

- Evens/odds
- Flip a coin

- Guess the number
- One potato
- Roll the highest number (dice or spinner)
- Bubble gum, bubble gum, in a dish
- Eeny-meeny-miney-moe
- Pick numbers out of a hat
- Draw straws
- Birthday person or person with closest birthday
- Youngest to oldest
- Tallest to shortest
- Draw names out of a hat
- Rock/paper/scissors

Activities

Practice and Learn a New One

Purpose: To introduce the children to new techniques for determining who goes first, and to discuss what to do if they do not get a chance to go first and how to deal with it.

Materials: Large paper for brainstorming, copies of "Who Goes First Chart" (found in Appendix B) for each group.

Preparation: Choose a way to figure out who goes first. Write up and make copies of the directions for the technique if appropriate.

Procedure:

1. After the children have brainstormed a list of ways to figure out who goes first, introduce a new way of doing so.

2. Split the children into groups of four and have them practice the new way. Have them use the technique five or six times and make a list of who was selected to go first.

3. Come together as a group and discuss how many times each person got to go first, and brainstorm as a group what to do if someone does not get a chance to go first.

Short Game Stations

Purpose: This is a great opportunity for children to practice figuring out who goes first. The object is to make this activity be about the different ways of going first and not the game itself.

Materials: Short games that take only a few minutes to play such as tic-tac-toe, Jenga, or Topple; timer

Preparation: Set up stations in different parts of the classroom so that only a few children are at a game at a time.

Procedure:

1. Describe the games that they are going to play at each station. Let the children know that they may not be able to finish the games, and that is okay. This is just a time to practice figuring out who goes first.

2. Have children be at each station for 3–5 minutes or enough time for them to figure out who goes first and start playing a game. Then have them switch to another station.

3. Come back together at the end and ask the children's opinion as to what method is best for figuring out who goes first.

Friendship Cards—Playing Games

Purpose: The friendship cards are used as a visual reminder for the children, to reinforce the concept that has been taught.

Materials: The following friendship card found in Appendix A:

- Ways to Figure Out Who Goes First

Preparation: See directions in "How to Use This Book."

Procedure: See directions in "How to Use This Book."

Generalization and Consistency

- When children are having a challenge remembering the strategies used, refer them back to their pack of friendship cards.
- Hang posters and concept maps and refer to them before children begin competitive games.

LESSON 3: HAPPY ENDINGS

Introduction/Overview

How we treat others in the face of winning and losing is at the heart of many of the conflicts that children have when playing competitive games. Many children get their feelings hurt when someone else wins a game and others are ridiculed if they win. In this lesson, we will discuss the way we treat others when we win and what we say and do if someone else wins. It is important to help the children see that having fun and challenging ourselves are the main goals of any game.

Teaching Concepts

- We play games to have fun.
- It is important to be a good sport at the end of a game.

Attitude

- The thrill of competing is as good if not better than winning itself.
- Children may need help seeing the positive outcomes when someone else wins.
- Winning is exciting and can be difficult to see past.

Lesson Objective

- Children will identify and use positive phrases and attitudes with their peers when they win a game.
- Children will identify and use positive phrases and attitudes with their peers when someone else wins a game.

Lesson Introduction

Concept Map—"Happy Endings"

Have the children help develop concept map by asking leading questions. Use the directions found in the "How to Use This Book" section.

Here are some suggestions for questions to ask:

- Why do we play games?
- At the end of the game

    - What do we say when we are the winner?

    - What do we say when someone else wins?

    - How do we say these things?

Activities

Try Trophy

Purpose: In this activity, we are emphasizing the importance of doing our best instead of winning.

Materials: Pint milk cartons, paper cups, pipe cleaners, construction paper, art supplies

Preparation: Cut the tops off the milk cartons. Wrap the milk cartons in construction paper.

Procedure:

1. Have children glue the paper cups on the top of their milk cartons.

2. Use pipe cleaners to make handles for the trophy.

3. Have children each write something (or write it for them) on the carton that they consider their strength when playing games. Add their names (glitter makes the names stand out).

Figure 6.1 Concept Map: Happy Endings

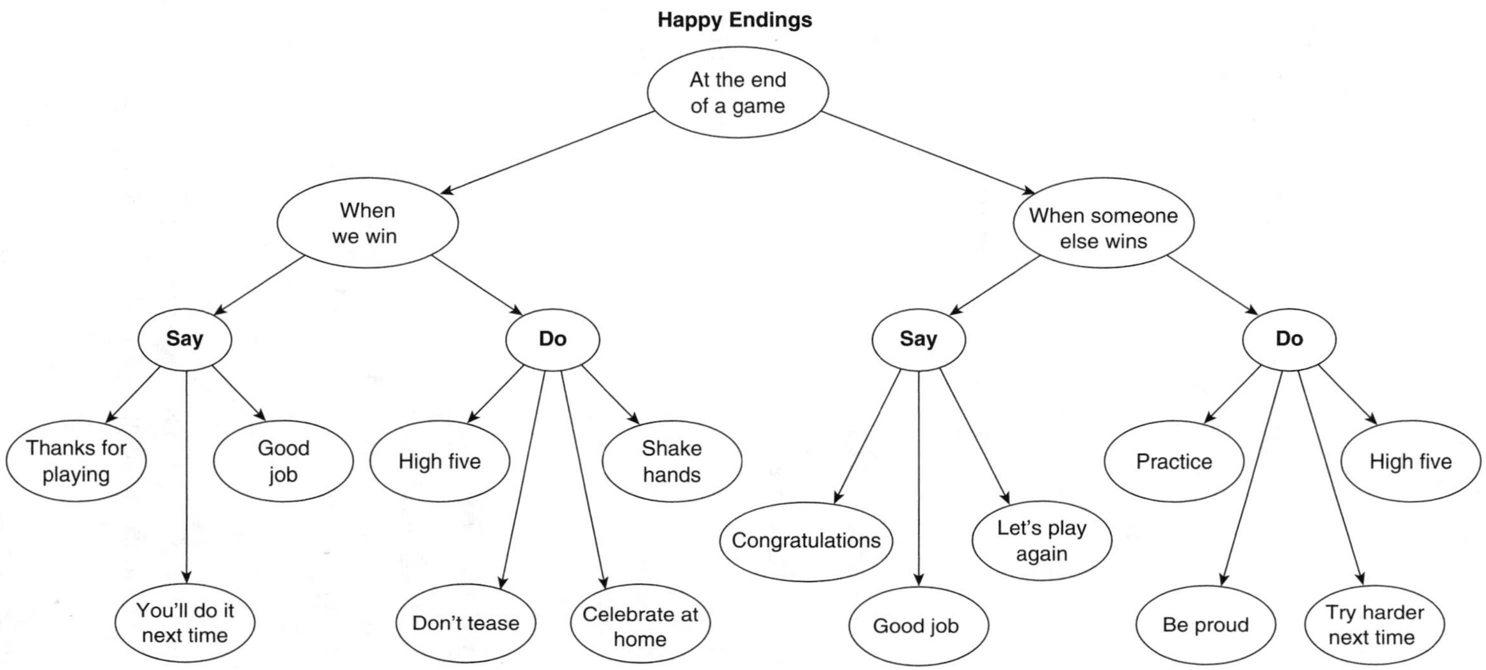

4. Have children decorate trophies with stickers, markers, and other art materials.

5. After trophies are dry, display them or have an award ceremony of strengths to build self-esteem.

Friendship Cards—Playing Games

Purpose: The friendship cards are used as a visual reminder for the children, to reinforce the concept that has been taught.

Materials: The following friendship card found in Appendix A:

- What We Say When We Win

Preparation: See directions in "How to Use This Book."

Procedure: See directions in "How to Use This Book."

LESSON 4: PLAYING FRIENDS' GAMES

Introduction/Overview

Many children become very rigid in the games they play. They also want to play the games the same way over and over. In this lesson, we will help children see the benefit of playing other people's games and playing them other ways. We will help them to internalize the concepts by showing them how much they benefit from playing friends' games.

Teaching Concepts

- Everyone has good ideas for games.
- It is fun to try new games and activities.
- We can try others things and still have it our way some of the time.

Attitude

- Many children are rigid because they are overwhelmed in a situation.
- Many children develop limited conceptions about how things "should" be done.

Lesson Objective

- Children will try new activities with peers.
- Children will teach peers new games that they enjoy.

Lesson Introduction

Brainstorm for Key Concepts

Have children develop lists to refer to by asking them specific questions. Use the directions found in the "How to Use This Book" section. Here are some suggestions of questions to ask:

- What games do you like to play?
- What games do you like to play with friends?
- Why do you want to play games with friends?
- Sometimes we don't want to play the other game. Why don't we want to?

Activities

The Games We Like Collage

Purpose: This activity is designed to help children get comfortable with the idea of playing other people's games. Many children get the idea that playing other people's games means that they don't get to play their own. In this activity, they will learn that they can both play others' games and sometimes play their own. Also we want to help the children to see the fun in playing others' games.

Materials: Large paper, toy catalogs, scissors, glue, markers

Preparation: Label a poster or large paper "Games I Like."

Procedure:

1. Share with the children that many times people like to play the same game, and their friend will want to play something that they will like.

2. Have children go through toy catalogs and make a collage of the games and toys they like.

3. Have each child show the poster he or she made.

4. Have the children switch the posters (in pairs) and take turns pointing out the games and toys on their friend's poster they like, too.

Change the Rules

Purpose: Children's rigidity can go as deep as the specific rules in a game. This activity is designed to help children be okay with little changes and understand that it doesn't change the fun of the game.

Materials: Have children bring their favorite game from home. Request from the parent that the game be a short one (can be played in 5–10 minutes).

Preparation: None

Procedure:

1. If working with a large group, split children into small groups of three or four.

2. Have one child explain the rules of his or her game to the rest of the group.

3. Everyone plays the game.

4. Then have each child, starting with the child who brought the game, think about one rule that can be changed. Write the rules down to help them remember.

5. Play the game again using the new rules.

6. After the game, talk about the game and the way the changed rules made it new and fun. Have children share which way was more fun. Remind them that rules can be changed and then changed back as often as they want as long as everyone agrees.

7. Go through the process again with another child's game.

Everyone Picks a Game and Explains How It Is Played

Purpose: In this activity, all children get an opportunity to play "their game" and share it with their friends. It also reinforces that other people's games are great to play and explore.

Materials: Games children bring from home

Preparation: Make a schedule with the children that outlines whose turn it is to bring a game in from home. For larger groups, split the children into groups of four or five.

Procedure:

1. Each child brings in a game from home or picks one from the class.

2. Have the children be in charge of explaining to the other children how the game is played.

3. Use the techniques from Lessons 2 and 3 for picking the child that goes first and happy endings.

4. After the game is played, have children share what they liked about the game.

Friendship Cards—Playing Games

Purpose: The friendship cards are used as a visual reminder for the children, to reinforce the concept that has been taught.

Materials: The following friendship card found in Appendix A:

- Why We Play Friends' Games

Preparation: See directions in "How to Use This Book."

Procedure: See directions in "How to Use This Book."

Generalization and Consistency

- Use picture schedules with pictures of the children in some group playtimes to illustrate how each child gets a turn picking the toy or game for the group. Pictures help children see that they will get their toy and their turn and make it easier for them to accept others' games.
- Refer children to the posters of why we play other people's game to help them remember what they learned from the experience of trying a new game.
- Refer children to the poster of what they like to play and have them pick toys and games that everyone enjoys.

LESSON 5: OUTDOOR GAMES

Introduction/Overview

At some point, all children will have an opportunity to play active games. In this lesson, we will go over the play vocabulary involved in outdoor games and sports and the body safety that is needed to make sure that all players have a fun and safe play time. One suggestion we have is to create a global policy about picking teams. To help children create positive attitudes about involving people regardless of ability, we suggest that you *do not allow children to have captains pick teams.* There are few people who do not have a negative experience about picking teams. We suggest eliminating this experience from your activities, especially if children are consistently having conflict over the process. Introduce the techniques in the first lesson as better ways to create teams.

Teaching Concepts

- Active games are great for everyone.
- Teamwork and good sportsmanship are the most important parts of sports.
- Even observers are a part of a sports game.
- Sport safety is essential.
- Everybody should be included and have fun.

Attitude

- Everyone can be a part of the action.

Lesson Objective

- Children will participate in sport and active games in a group setting.
- Children will try a new aspect of active games.

Lesson Introduction

Brainstorm for Key Concepts

Have children develop lists to refer to by asking them specific questions. Use the directions found in the "How to Use This Book" section.

- Brainstorm types of sports games.
- Brainstorm outdoor safety rules.

Activities

Positive Team Picking

Purpose: In this activity, we are helping children to build positive alternatives for picking teams that include all children. The purpose is to introduce the children to new techniques for picking teams and to discuss what to do if they do not get picked and how to deal with it.

Materials: Two pieces of large paper for brainstorming, posters or art paper, art supplies

Preparation: None

Procedure:

1. Start by discussing with the children how it feels to be left out of a game.

2. Have children brainstorm a list of ways to create teams without having captains picking. Here are two examples:

   a. Count off by twos.
   b. Pick names from a hat.

3. Split children into groups or have them work individually. Have children create posters about including all friends in their games. Have children include in the poster one of the suggestions for how to pick teams.

4. Hang posters and refer to them on a daily basis.

Soccer

Purpose: This is a good game to teach children. The rules can be simplified for any age and limitation. It is also helpful for creating body strength and muscle tone.

Materials: Soccerball, something to use as goals, score sheet

Preparation: Set up field for soccer game.

Procedure:

1. Have children practice kicking the ball around the field, stopping them frequently to give pointers and suggestions.

2. After children have practiced, split them into teams and begin keeping score.

3. At the end of the game, use this as an opportunity to review happy endings and use the skills they were introduced to in that lesson.

Shooting Baskets—Indoor/Outdoor Around the World

Purpose: Many games or simple outdoor activities can involve shooting baskets. It can be a source of anxiety for children who do not have the experience doing it. Practice is the only way to develop the ability to shoot baskets, and it is worth encouraging children to do. Around the World is a simple game that encourages children to go at their own speed. It can be played in teams with the object of the entire team finishing.

Materials: Basketball (for indoors, use a Nerf basketball, and a laundry basket), paper or other method to mark the various "stations" around the world.

Preparation: Around a basketball hoop outdoors, mark five stations in a half-circle, with the third one being directly in front of the basket. Make sure to put the markers at a distance appropriate for the children. Indoors, set desks in a circle around the laundry basket. Mark five or six "stations" around the world by taping pieces of paper to various desks spaced around the circle.

Procedure:

1. Tell children they will need to sink a basket from each "station" around the world. In the indoor game, have children stand behind the desks or sit on top of them.

2. Split children into teams and have the goal be for the whole team to finish, to lengthen the game for less skilled shooters.

3. Encourage children to play on the playground in their free time to practice their skill.

Relay Race

Purpose: This is an activity that was used in Lesson 1 of this unit, but is very relevant to this lesson, so we suggest using it again. This can be a good time to also do the challenge relay race again (see Lesson 1), to point out the need to sometimes change games to meet friends' physical needs.

Materials: Spoons, golf balls, pom-pom balls, balloons

Preparation: Have children split into groups. Set up course.

Procedure:

1. Line up groups of children to run relay races.

2. Each child needs to run down and back with the ball on the spoon without dropping the ball. If the child drops the ball, he or she has to start over.

3. Start by having children use the heaviest ball (it will stay on the spoon the best).

4. With each race, introduce a new ball or the balloon.

5. Remind the children that they need to pay attention to their bodies and comment if someone becomes too crazy or wild and needs to gain some control.

6. Also point out when someone is going too slowly and can speed up.

Friendship Cards—Playing Games

Purpose: The friendship cards are used as a visual reminder for the children, to reinforce the concept that has been taught.

Materials: The following friendship card found in Appendix A:

- Ways to Be Safe Outside

Preparation: See directions in "How to Use This Book."

Procedure: See directions in "How to Use This Book."

Generalization and Consistency

- Refer children to friendship cards when they are having conflicts.
- Plan times of being on the playground or other outdoor play setting to facilitate children and make sure the skills taught are being implemented.

LESSON 6: INDOOR GAMES

Introduction/Overview

It benefits all children to develop a love of board games. Board and card games are a great way to help children develop interactive skills such as sharing, waiting for a turn, communicating, and conflict resolution. Traditionally, dramatic play is usually only addressed in the early childhood years. We chose to include this in our elementary curriculum because many children have difficulties in playing pretend that are not noticed until well into kindergarten, and they continue to be a challenge throughout first to third grade where children still dabble in the dramatics. In this unit, we try to reinforce the children's understanding of playing pretend and set up dramatic scenes for children to practice with others.

Many children with special needs are concrete thinkers and are drawn to building and construction. However, they can have difficulty with the social needs in these types of situations. In this lesson, we will introduce the children to the vocabulary and safety issues involved when working with others on construction projects.

Teaching Concepts

- There are many rules in board games that make them fun and challenging.
- Everyone must agree to the rules to play the game.
- Communicating verbally is the key to avoiding conflicts with others.

Attitude

- Children may have difficulty with self-control in open play and need patience to help them work out conflicts.
- It is easy for children to get overwhelmed with the sensory stimulation in open play indoors, and they will need sensory input.

Lesson Objective

- Children will interact with peers in a safe way in a variety of indoor games.
- Children will come up with dramatic play themes with peers.
- Children will play board games appropriately.

Lesson Introduction

Brainstorm for Key Concepts

Have children develop lists to refer to by asking them specific questions. Use the directions found in the "How to Use This Book" section. Here are some suggestions of questions to ask:

- What do we play indoors?
- How do we play board games?
- How do we have fun with friends in pretend play?
- How do we build safely?

Activities

Restaurant Dramatic Play

Purpose: This activity may be too simple for children who are in the elementary grades, but it should still be considered as an option. Pretend play is difficult for some children who are concrete thinkers to grasp. Dramatic play experiences are wonderful opportunities for working on relating to others, social language, and problem-solving skills.

Materials: Play food, dishes, paper and art supplies, costumes, space with tables and chairs

Preparation: If necessary, brainstorm with the children the things they would see in a restaurant, and make a sequence of what happens when they go to a restaurant using a "What Happens Next?" worksheet found in Appendix B.

Figure 6.2   Restaurant Sequence

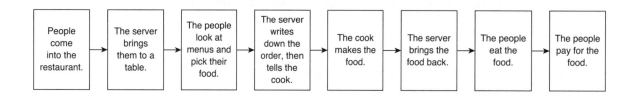

Procedure:

1. Have children pick who they want to be in the restaurant setting.

2. Have them act out the sequence of events that happens when they go to a restaurant.

3. Facilitate by staying back and observing and suggesting ideas when the play starts to slow down.

4. If children are extremely challenged, take a role in the play and model how to be involved and pretend to be a part.

Building Challenge

Purpose: In this challenge, the children are asked to work together with building materials and interact with other children in a safe way. The skills needed for building and construction in a group setting are used throughout the school years in classroom projects.

Materials: Building materials such as blocks, tinker toys, or Lincoln logs; plastic cup; small blocks or marbles to use as weights in the cup

Preparation: Review the rules with the children that were introduced in the Safe Body lesson in Unit 3. Brainstorm a list of things that we also need to remember to keep our bodies safe when playing with building materials. Here are some examples:

- Keep materials on the floor or table (no throwing).
- Hand things to our friends.
- Watch our hands and feet so we don't knock things over.
- Ask before we knock someone's project down.

Procedure:

1. Split children into groups and distribute building materials so all groups have about the same amount.

2. Tell the children that they need to build a tower that is very strong and can support the weight of the plastic cup with the weights inside.

3. Observe the children as they build, facilitating them through any conflicts.

4. When they are finished building, warn the children that the buildings might fall and assure them that if they do, you will help them rebuild. Put the cup on the top of each building and add a set amount of weights to the cup to see if the tower can support it. After each building is tested, ask the children if they want to see how much the buildings can hold until they fall down. (Note: Do not suggest this if any of the children have difficulties with construction falling down.)

5. Extra challenge: Add a height requirement to the building instructions such as it must be at least one foot high and support the weight.

Life-Size Board Game

Purpose: This activity can be played during the centers activity as one of the centers once it is created. This is a great activity for helping children with the directional aspect of board games. Physically creating the game and acting it out help children internalize the aspects of playing board games.

Materials: Polyspots, index cards, pint milk cartons, markers

Preparation: Wrap milk cartons in white paper.

Procedure:

1. Brainstorm rules for a board game.

2. Have children brainstorm the different things that can happen in a board game when you land on a particular spot (examples: Go ahead two spaces, go back two spaces, take another turn, lose a turn).

3. Have children lay out polyspots in a path with a beginning and an end, and color dots on the milk cartons to make dice

4. Write the rules/directions that the children brainstormed on cards and have them tape them on the "board." Include a "start," "finish," and cards with arrows drawn on them to help children with direction of play.

5. Using the milk carton dice, play the game using the children as the game pieces.

Create Your Own Board Game

Purpose: Similar to the Life-Size Board Game, this activity will give children a hands-on experience with the ins and outs of board game playing.

Materials: Old board game, art materials, materials needed for the specific parts of the game based on the children's brainstorming, Brainstorming Project Sheets in Appendix B.

Preparation:

1. Glue paper on the top of the board game to cover its original artwork.

2. Help children build an awareness of the different parts of the board game by starting with a concept map.

Concept Map—"What Are the Parts of a Board Game?"

Have the children help develop a concept map by asking them leading questions. Use the directions found in the "How to Use This Book" section.

Figure 6.3   Concept Map: Board Games

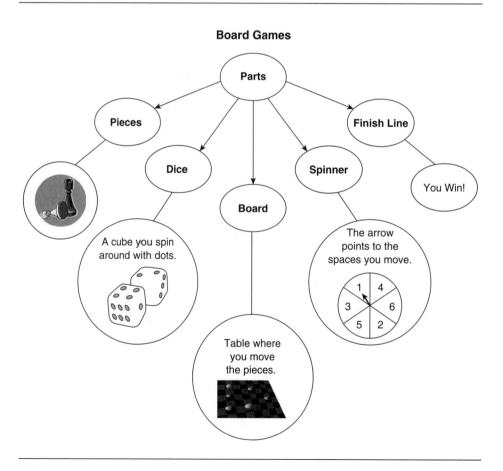

Procedure:

1. As a group, have the children think of a theme for the game. Encourage them to be as crazy and creative as they can. Decide how many players, whether to use dice or spinner or both, how many dice to use, etc.

2. Split the group into teams to work on the different parts of the game. Have the children use the project sheet to help them plan what they need to do to create the section of the game they are responsible for.

3. Based on the brainstorming, collect the materials needed. Suggestions: clay for creating the game pieces, wood blocks for dice, paper plates for spinners, etc.

4. Have children work on project, checking on them periodically as they progress.

5. When game is finished, have the children play in teams. This is a good time to add it to the centers.

Centers

Purpose: The purpose of the centers is to set up a natural environment where the children are exploring play together. This is a wonderful culmination activity for children to use all they have learned.

Materials: Activity materials and toys available

Preparation: Set up a space that has tabletop games, building areas, dramatic play space, and places for art and reading.

Procedure:

1. Have planned time in the day when children can interact in the centers space and can be supported by an adult. This is an opportunity to allow children some extra time to try the skills taught and even allow them to use the wrong strategy, giving them the chance to self-correct.

Friendship Cards–Playing Games

Purpose: The friendship cards are used as a visual reminder for the children, to reinforce the concept that has been taught.

Materials: The following friendship card found in Appendix A:

- Parts of a Board Game

Preparation: See directions in "How to Use This Book."

Procedure: See directions in "How to Use This Book."

Generalization and Consistency

- Post rules that have been developed with each of the lessons.
- Refer children to friendship cards when they are having conflicts.
- Remember the importance of planned, structured, facilitated play days.

Appendix A

Friendship Cards—Master List

Unit 1—Discovering Friendships

- Friendship
- Why Friends Are Great
- Ways to Say Hello
- Ways to Introduce Yourself
- Ways to Show Appreciation
- Things We Can Find Out About Friends
- Our Friends
- How Our Friends Act

Unit 2—Using Eye Contact

- Why We Look at Other People
- Why Other People Look at Us
- Where We Look When We Are Talking
- Why We Look at the Eyes When We Are Talking
- How Looking Helps Us to Listen
- What We Learn From Looking
- What We Do With Others
- Why We Have Friends

Unit 3—Being a Friend

- What You Do to Be a Good Friend
- Sweet Words You Can Use
- Why We Use Sweet/Kind Words With Our Friends
- Why We Keep Our Bodies Safe
- Why We Keep Our Friends' Bodies Safe
- How We Use Our Hands/Feet
- How We Use Our Bodies
- What We Do Together to Play and Have Fun

Unit 4—Appropriate Body

- My Personal Space
- What We Say if Someone Is in Our Personal Space
- Things We Do to Respect Our Friends' Body Privacy
- What I Do if Someone Invades My Body Privacy
- What We Do in the Morning to Be Neat and Clean
- What We Do During the Day to Be Neat and Clean
- What We Do at Night to Be Neat and Clean
- How We Slow Our Body When It Is Too Fast
- How We Get Our Body Moving When It Is Too Slow
- Places for Fast Body Speed
- Places for Slow Body Speed
- Places for Focused Body
- Things I Do Well
- Things I Need Help With
- People Who Help Me

Unit 5—Interacting in a Group

- Interested Face
- Listening Body
- Ways We Learn in a Group
- Circle Time/Meeting Time
- Words to Use When Sharing Ideas
- Ways to Get Someone's Attention

Unit 6—Playing Games

- A Good Sport
- Ways to Cheer Your Friends
- Ways to Figure Out Who Goes First
- What We Say When We Win
- What We Say When Someone Else Wins
- Why We Play Friends' Games
- Ways to Be Safe Outside
- Parts of a Board Game

the
WANNA PLAY
program
This pack of
friendship
cards belongs
to:

_____

Unit 1 – Discovering Friendships
Friendship

❖

❖

❖

the
WANNA PLAY
program

Unit 1 – Discovering Friendships
Why Friends Are Great

❖

❖

❖

the
WANNA PLAY
program

Unit 1 – Discovering Friendships
Ways to Say Hello

❖

❖

❖

the
WANNA PLAY
program

Unit 1 – Discovering Friendships
Ways to Introduce Yourself

❖

❖

❖

the
WANNA PLAY
program

Unit 1 – Discovering Friendships
Ways to Show Appreciation

❖

❖

❖

the
WANNA PLAY
program

Unit 1 – Discovering Friendships
Things We Can Find Out About Friends

❖

❖

❖

the **WANNA PLAY** program

Unit 1 – Discovering Friendships
Our Friends

❖

❖

❖

the **WANNA PLAY** program

Unit 1 – Discovering Friendships
How Our Friends Act

❖

❖

❖

the **WANNA PLAY** program

Unit 2 – Using Eye Contact
Why We Look at Other People

❖

❖

❖

the **WANNA PLAY** program

Unit 2 – Using Eye Contact
Why Other People Look at Us

❖

❖

❖

the **WANNA PLAY** program

Unit 2 – Using Eye Contact
Where We Look When We Are Talking

❖

❖

❖

the **WANNA PLAY** program

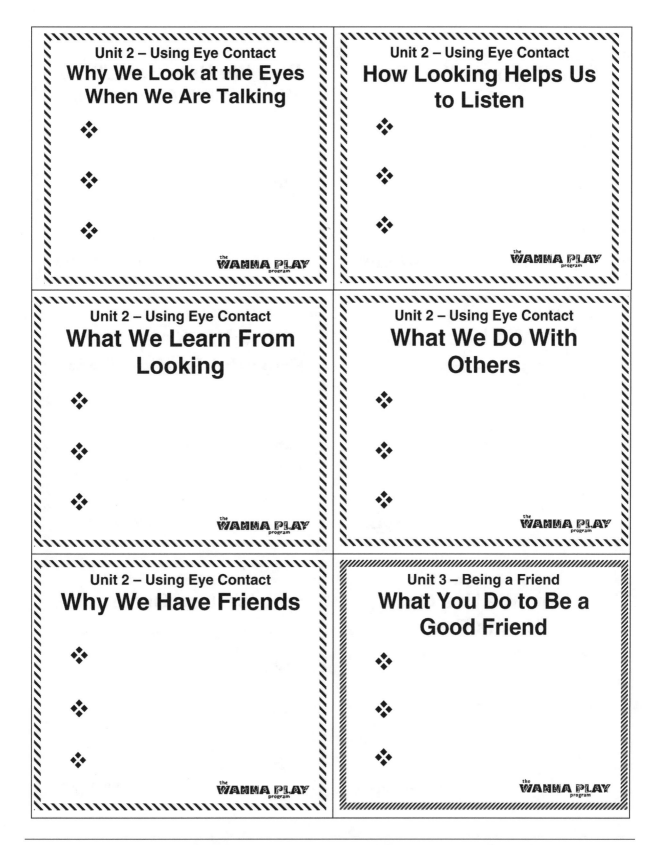

Unit 2 – Using Eye Contact
Why We Look at the Eyes When We Are Talking

❖

❖

❖

the WANNA PLAY program

Unit 2 – Using Eye Contact
How Looking Helps Us to Listen

❖

❖

❖

the WANNA PLAY program

Unit 2 – Using Eye Contact
What We Learn From Looking

❖

❖

❖

the WANNA PLAY program

Unit 2 – Using Eye Contact
What We Do With Others

❖

❖

❖

the WANNA PLAY program

Unit 2 – Using Eye Contact
Why We Have Friends

❖

❖

❖

the WANNA PLAY program

Unit 3 – Being a Friend
What You Do to Be a Good Friend

❖

❖

❖

the WANNA PLAY program

Unit 3 – Being a Friend
Sweet Words You Can Use

❖

❖

❖

the WANNA PLAY program

Unit 3 – Being a Friend
Why We Use Sweet/Kind Words With Our Friends

❖

❖

❖

the WANNA PLAY program

Unit 3 – Being a Friend
Why We Keep Our Bodies Safe

❖

❖

❖

the WANNA PLAY program

Unit 3 – Being a Friend
Why We Keep Our Friends' Bodies Safe

❖

❖

❖

the WANNA PLAY program

Unit 3 – Being a Friend
How We Use Our Hands/Feet

❖

❖

❖

the WANNA PLAY program

Unit 3 – Being a Friend
How We Use Our Bodies

❖

❖

❖

the WANNA PLAY program

Unit 3 – Being a Friend
What We Do Together to Play and Have Fun

❖

❖

❖

the WANNA PLAY
program

Unit 4 – Appropriate Body
My Personal Space

the WANNA PLAY
program

Unit 4 – Appropriate Body
What We Say if Someone Is in Our Personal Space

❖

❖

❖

the WANNA PLAY
program

Unit 4 – Appropriate Body
Things We Do to Respect Our Friends' Body Privacy

❖

❖

❖

the WANNA PLAY
program

Unit 4 – Appropriate Body
What I Do if Someone Invades My Body Privacy

❖

❖

❖

the WANNA PLAY
program

Unit 4 – Appropriate Body
What We Do in the Morning to Be Neat and Clean

❖

❖

❖

the WANNA PLAY
program

Unit 4 – Appropriate Body
What We Do During the Day to Be Neat and Clean

❖

❖

❖

the
WANNA PLAY
program

Unit 4 – Appropriate Body
What We Do at Night to Be Neat and Clean

❖

❖

❖

the
WANNA PLAY
program

Unit 4 – Appropriate Body
How We Slow Our Body When It Is Too Fast

❖

❖

❖

the
WANNA PLAY
program

Unit 4 – Appropriate Body
How We Get Our Body Moving When It Is Too Slow

❖

❖

❖

the
WANNA PLAY
program

Unit 4 – Appropriate Body
Places for Fast Body Speed

❖

❖

❖

the
WANNA PLAY
program

Unit 4 – Appropriate Body
Places for Slow Body Speed

❖

❖

❖

the
WANNA PLAY
program

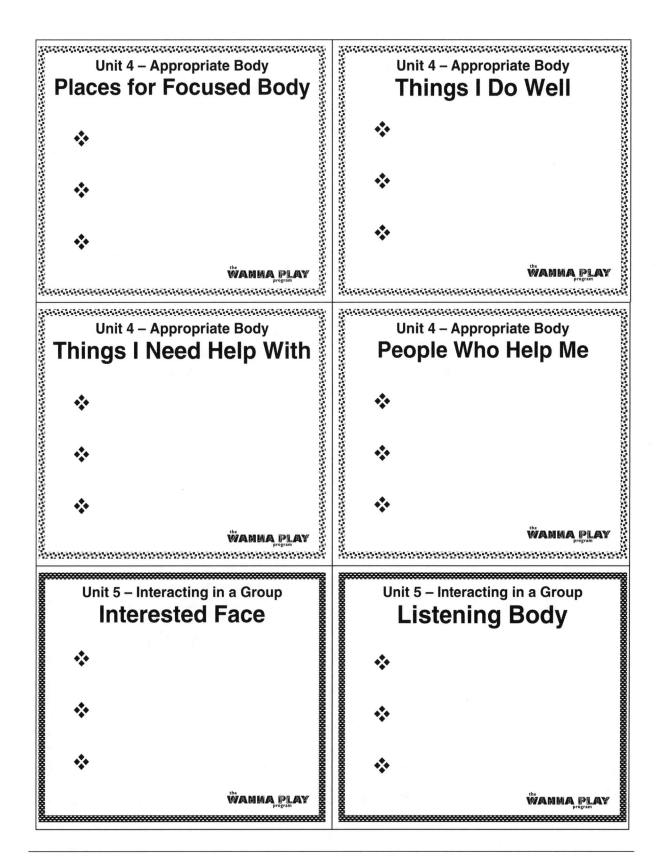

Unit 4 – Appropriate Body
Places for Focused Body

❖

❖

❖

the WANNA PLAY program

Unit 4 – Appropriate Body
Things I Do Well

❖

❖

❖

the WANNA PLAY program

Unit 4 – Appropriate Body
Things I Need Help With

❖

❖

❖

the WANNA PLAY program

Unit 4 – Appropriate Body
People Who Help Me

❖

❖

❖

the WANNA PLAY program

Unit 5 – Interacting in a Group
Interested Face

❖

❖

❖

the WANNA PLAY program

Unit 5 – Interacting in a Group
Listening Body

❖

❖

❖

the WANNA PLAY program

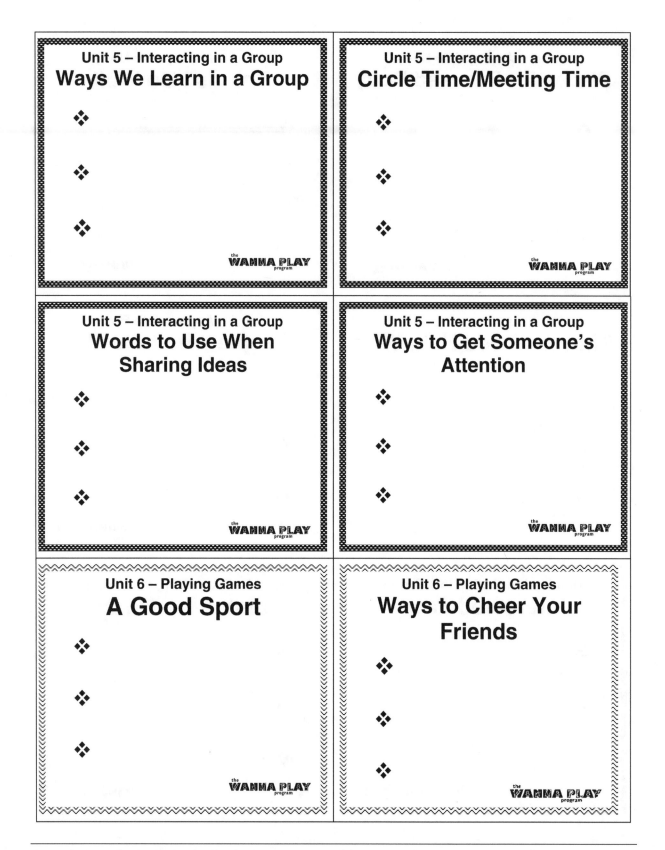

Unit 5 – Interacting in a Group
Ways We Learn in a Group

❖

❖

❖

the WANNA PLAY program

Unit 5 – Interacting in a Group
Circle Time/Meeting Time

❖

❖

❖

the WANNA PLAY program

Unit 5 – Interacting in a Group
Words to Use When Sharing Ideas

❖

❖

❖

the WANNA PLAY program

Unit 5 – Interacting in a Group
Ways to Get Someone's Attention

❖

❖

❖

the WANNA PLAY program

Unit 6 – Playing Games
A Good Sport

❖

❖

❖

the WANNA PLAY program

Unit 6 – Playing Games
Ways to Cheer Your Friends

❖

❖

❖

the WANNA PLAY program

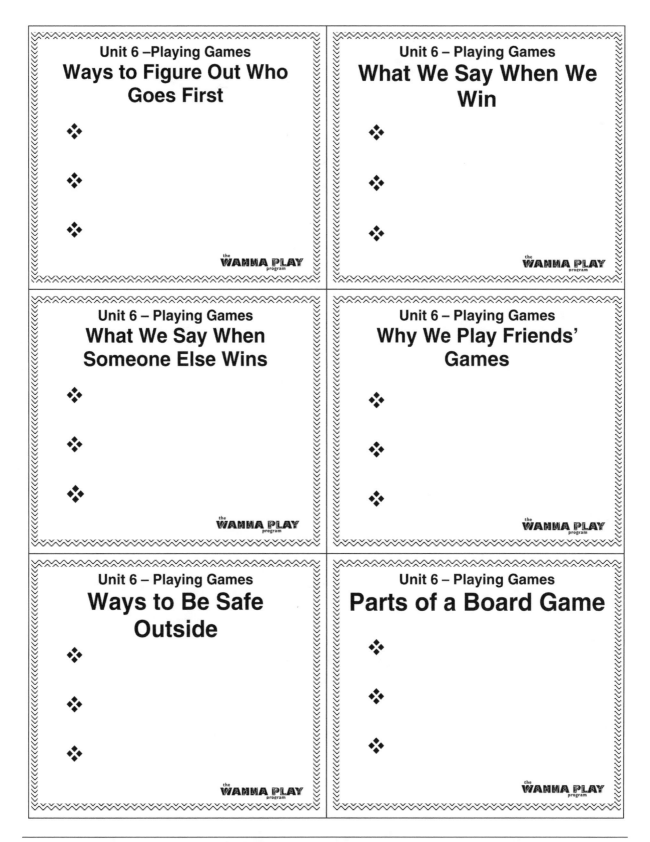

Unit 6 –Playing Games
Ways to Figure Out Who Goes First

❖

❖

❖

the **WANNA PLAY** program

Unit 6 – Playing Games
What We Say When We Win

❖

❖

❖

the **WANNA PLAY** program

Unit 6 – Playing Games
What We Say When Someone Else Wins

❖

❖

❖

the **WANNA PLAY** program

Unit 6 – Playing Games
Why We Play Friends' Games

❖

❖

❖

the **WANNA PLAY** program

Unit 6 – Playing Games
Ways to Be Safe Outside

❖

❖

❖

the **WANNA PLAY** program

Unit 6 – Playing Games
Parts of a Board Game

❖

❖

❖

the **WANNA PLAY** program

Appendix B

Worksheets Master List

Unit 1—Discovering Friendships

- Making Friends
- You and Your Friend
- Friendship Quilt
- Best Friends Worksheet
- School Friends Worksheet
- Friend Bingo
- Gift of Friendship Worksheet
- Letter to a Friend
- People Flashcards
- Place Flashcards

Unit 2—Using Eye Contact

- Paper Doll Worksheet
- Paper Doll Clothes
- Silly Glasses Worksheet
- Picture Flashcards
- Social Phrases Flashcards
- Puppets for "Brown Bear"
- Emotion Bingo
- Emotion Flashcards
- Eye Coloring Sheet
- Who's It Going to Be?

Unit 3—Being a Friend

- Safe Body
- "Safe Body" Doll Clothes

- Friendship Train
- Situation Flashcards

Unit 4—Appropriate Body Behavior

- Appropriate Pyramid
- Washing Our Hands

Unit 5—Interacting in a Group

- Brainstorm for a Group Project
- Clue Flashcards
- Goop
- Group Meeting Notes
- Group Project To-Do List
- Interested Face

Unit 6—Playing Games

- "Who Goes First?" Chart
- Copy the Picture
- Score Sheet 1
- Score Sheet 2
- What Happens Next?

Making
Friends

Making Friends

Your new friend's name:

_____

Where do you see him or her?

_____

What could you say to try to make friends?

_____

_____

What are some things you could do together?

_____

_____

Why do you want to be the person's friend?

_____

_____

You and Your Friend

Friendship Quilt

Best Friends Worksheet

Copyright © 2007 by Corwin Press. All rights reserved. Reprinted from *Wanna Play: Friendship Skills for Preschool and Elementary Grades*, by Ruth Herron Ross and Beth Roberts-Pacchione. Thousand Oaks, CA: Corwin Press, www.corwinpress.com. Reproduction authorized only for the local school site or nonprofit organization that has purchased this book.

School Friends Worksheet

Friend Bingo

Been to another country	Has a pet	Likes the color green	Likes to eat pizza
Has a brother or sister	Is going to the beach this summer	Likes to read	Saw/Read Harry Potter
Has a GameBoy	Likes to ride a bike	Shares a room with a brother or sister	Is in third grade
Likes to eat ice cream	Can blow bubbles with bubble gum	Has been to an amusement park	Can hop on one foot

Gift of Friendship Worksheet

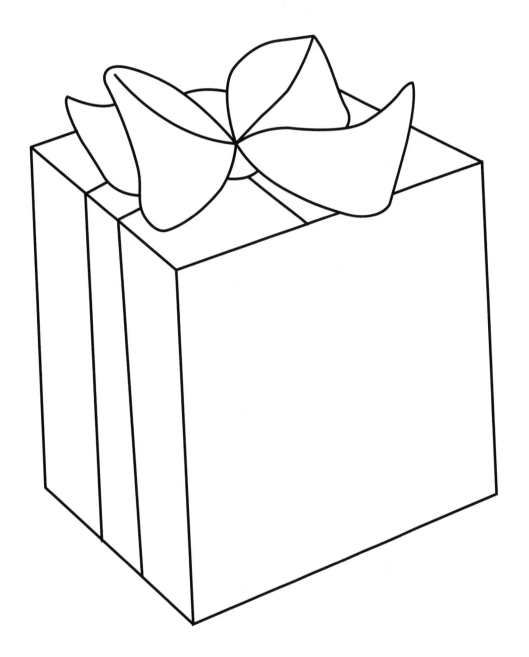

Letter to a Friend

Dear _____,

    I enjoyed being in your class this year.

    I really liked playing _____.

    Do you remember when we _____

_____? Would you like to play

_____ with me?

    Here is a picture of us together.

    Hope I see you soon!

    Your friend,

    _____

People Flashcards

People Flashcards   (Continued)

Grandmother	Grandfather
Principal	Neighbor
Fire Person	Cashier at Store
Aunt	Uncle

Place Flashcards

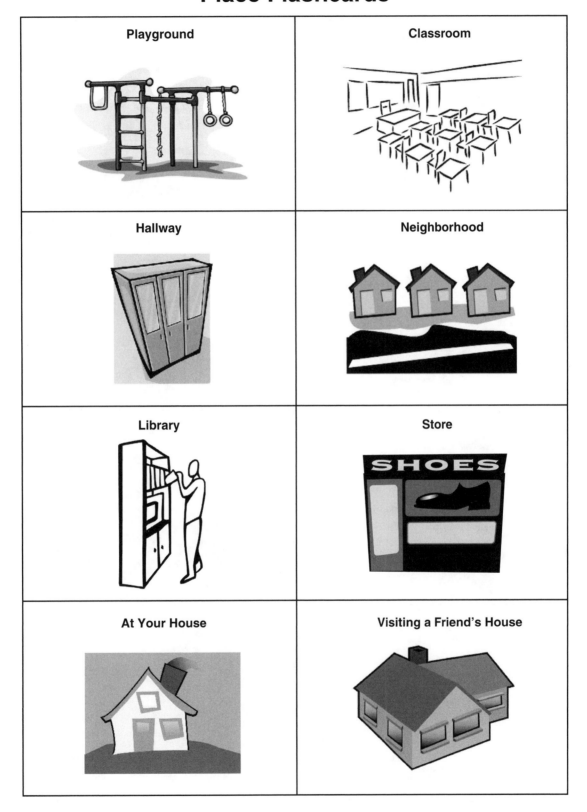

Playground	Classroom
Hallway	Neighborhood
Library	Store
At Your House	Visiting a Friend's House

Place Flashcards   (Continued)

At McDonald's	At the Movies
At the Beach	**At a Basketball Game**
At Recess	**In Your Backyard**

Paper Doll Worksheet

Paper Doll Clothes

Silly Glasses Worksheet

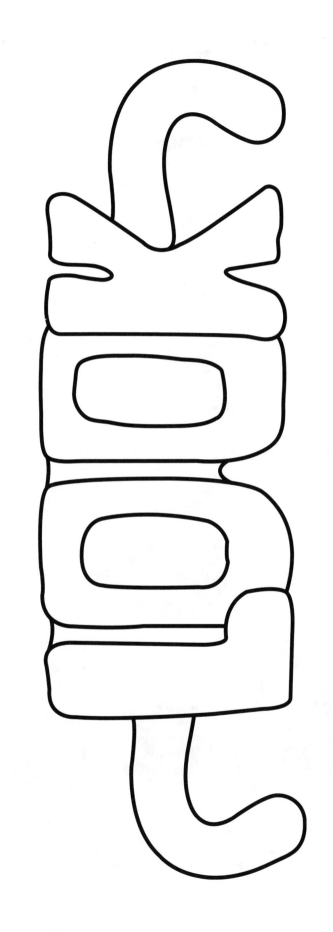

Picture Flashcards

Crayons	Paint set	Telephone
TV	Book	Trampoline
Bike	Ball	Baseball
Board game	Game Boy	Blocks

Picture Flashcards (Continued)

Sailboat	Sand castle	Fish
Shovel and bucket	Ladybug	Birthday cake
Birthday present	Pizza	Hot dog
Ice cream	Popcorn	Pancakes

Picture Flashcards (Continued)

Apple	Tree	Flower
Swing set	Camera	Lunchbox/Lunch bag
Doll	Toy car	Train
Skates	Skateboard	Guitar

Picture Flashcards (Continued)

Drums	Legos	Lollypop

Social Phrases Flashcards

How can I help you?	**How are you?**
Can I have that?	**Will you hand me that?**
Thank you.	**Hi!**
You're welcome.	**I'm sorry.**
I didn't mean to do that.	**Can I try again?**

Social Phrases Flashcards (Continued)

How old are you?	**God bless you.**
Excuse me.	**Do you want to come to my house?**
No thanks.	**Please wait your turn.**
Wait a minute please.	**Please leave me alone.**
Please move over.	**Please don't hit me.**

Social Phrases Flashcards (Continued)

Can I have that back?	**You look nice today.**
Listen to me, please.	**I need your help.**
Good-bye.	**See you later.**
What are you doing?	**Can I go first?**
It's your turn.	

Puppets for "Brown Bear"

Puppets for "Brown Bear" (Continued)

Puppets for "Brown Bear" (Continued)

Puppets for "Brown Bear" (Continued)

Puppets for "Brown Bear" (Continued)

Emotion Bingo

Emotion Bingo (Continued)

Silly	Scared	Talkative
Mad	Happy	Curious
Enbarrassed	Nervous	Sad

Emotion Bingo (Continued)

Emotion Bingo (Continued)

Calm	Surprised	Sneaky
Proud	Happy	Shy
Sleepy	Confused	Silly

Emotion Flashcards

HAPPY	**CALM**
SURPRISED	**SNEAKY**
PROUD	**SHY**
SLEEPY	**CONFUSED**

Emotion Flashcards (Continued)

SILLY	**SCARED**
TALKATIVE	**MAD**
CURIOUS	**EMBARRASSED**
NERVOUS	**SAD**

Eye Coloring Sheet

Who's It Going to Be?

Who do you want to . . .

Sit with on the bus on a school trip? _____

Be in a group project with? _____

Be on a deserted island with? _____

Invite over to your house? _____

Go to the movies with? _____

Talk about your problems with? _____

Play video games with? _____

Play your favorite sport with? _____

Do homework with? _____

Hang out at their house with? _____

Eat lunch with? _____

"Safe Body" Doll Clothes

Friendship Train

Situation Flashcards

You are asking a friend to play.	**You are asking a teacher to help you with homework.**
You are hungry and you want your mom to get you something to eat.	**You want a turn with a toy that your friend is playing with.**
A friend took your toy without asking.	**You want to watch TV for five more minutes when you are told to turn it off.**
A friend is talking too loudly and you want to ask him or her to talk quieter.	**Someone hits you.**

Situation Flashcards (Continued)

You don't understand what someone has just said and you want to ask the person to repeat it.	There is a new student in class and you want to say hello.
You are playing a game with friends and they skip your turn. Tell them that they skipped you and you want your turn.	You are finished playing what everyone else is playing and you want to do something new.
You just stepped on your friend's foot by accident.	You want to go first.
Your friends are playing a game and you want to play, too.	

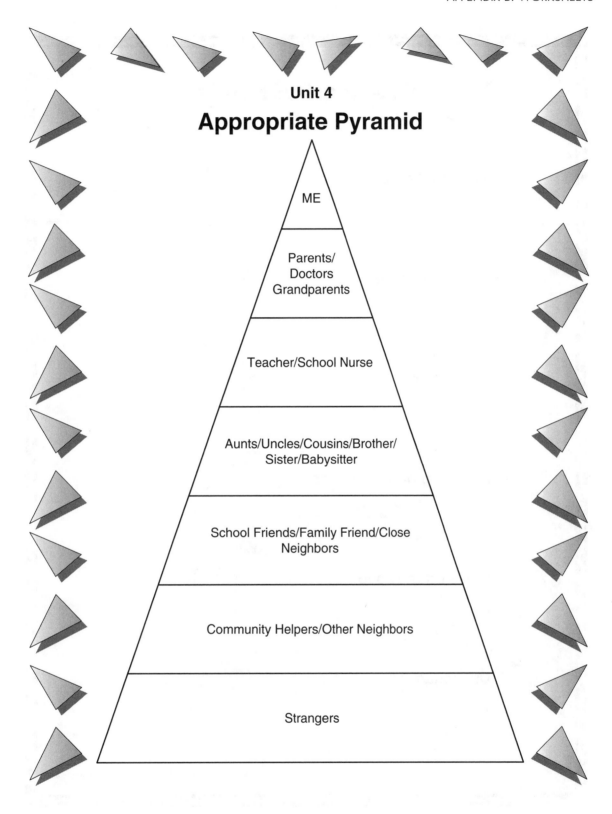

Unit 4
Appropriate Pyramid

ME

Parents/
Doctors
Grandparents

Teacher/School Nurse

Aunts/Uncles/Cousins/Brother/
Sister/Babysitter

School Friends/Family Friend/Close
Neighbors

Community Helpers/Other Neighbors

Strangers

Washing Our Hands

1. Turn on the water

2. Wet your hands

3. Get the soap

4. Rub soap on your hands

5. Rinse off the soap

6. Dry hands

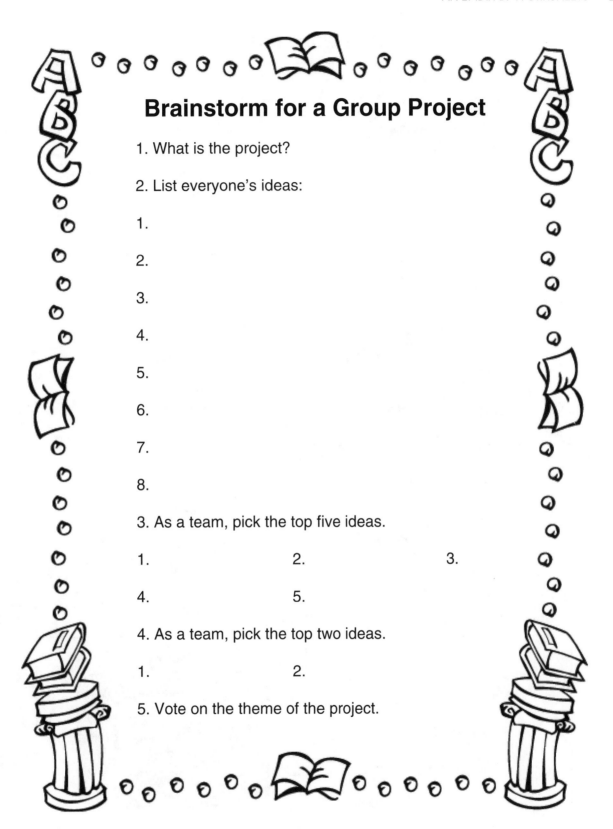

Brainstorm for a Group Project

1. What is the project?

2. List everyone's ideas:

1.

2.

3.

4.

5.

6.

7.

8.

3. As a team, pick the top five ideas.

1.   2.   3.

4.   5.

4. As a team, pick the top two ideas.

1.   2.

5. Vote on the theme of the project.

Clue Flashcards

Sauce Set 1	**Brush** Set 2
Cheese Set 1	**Paint** Set 2
Dough Set 1	**Paper** Set 2
Pizza Set 1	**Picture** Set 2

Clue Flashcards (Continued)

Bubbles	Leaf
Set 3	Set 4
Can	Branch
Set 3	Set 4
Straw	Nest
Set 3	Set 4
Soda	Tree
Set 3	Set 4

Clue Flashcards (Continued)

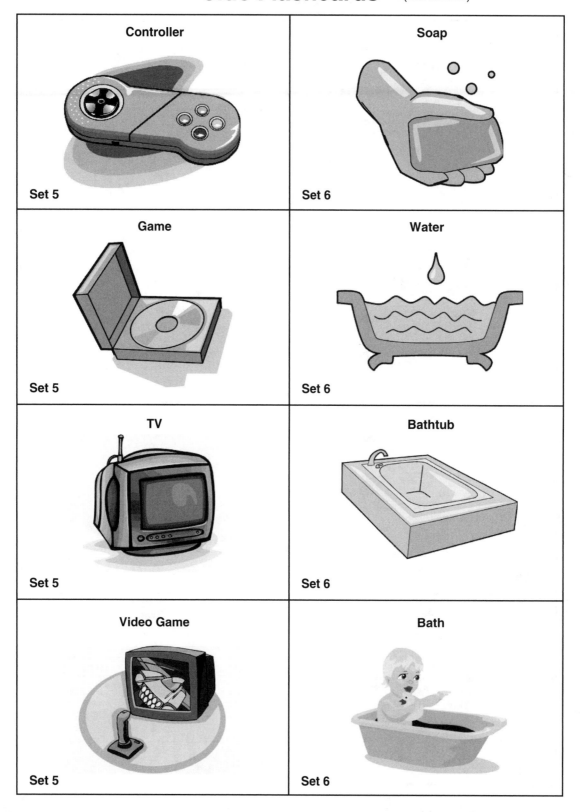

Controller — Set 5	**Soap** — Set 6
Game — Set 5	**Water** — Set 6
TV — Set 5	**Bathtub** — Set 6
Video Game — Set 5	**Bath** — Set 6

Clue Flashcards (Continued)

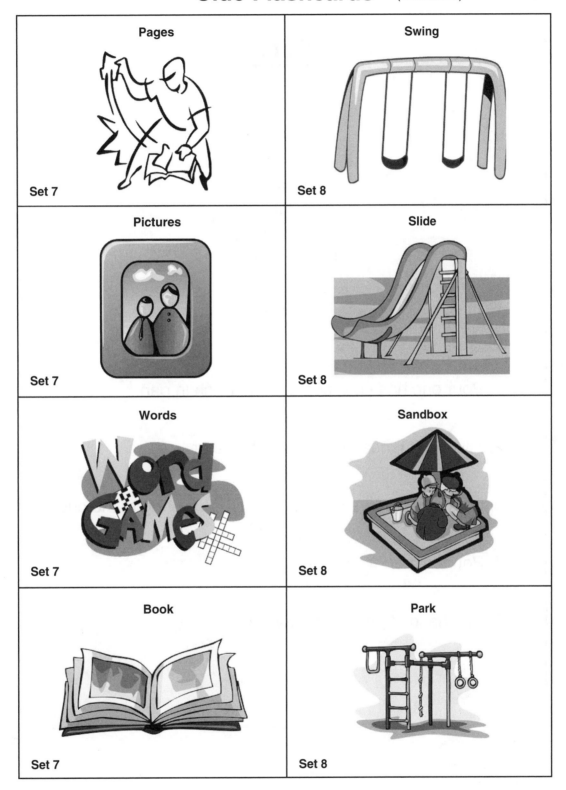

Pages	**Swing**
Set 7	Set 8
Pictures	**Slide**
Set 7	Set 8
Words	**Sandbox**
Set 7	Set 8
Book	**Park**
Set 7	Set 8

Goop

You will need:

Cornstarch
Water
Pan
Measuring cups
Food coloring

Directions:

1. Pour one half (1/2) cup of cornstarch in pan.

2. Fill one (1) measuring cup with water.

3. Have adult add three drops of food coloring to the cup.

4. Pour colored water into pan.

5. Use hands to mix and play with goop. ☺

Group Meeting Notes

Date of meeting: _____

What is completed?

1.

2.

3.

4.

5.

What needs to be completed?

Who will do this? _____

Who will do this? _____

Group Project To-Do List

Name of project: _____

To-do list:

1.

2.

3.

4.

List each person's job:

Name:_____ 1.
2.
3.

Name:_____ 1.
2.
3.

Name:_____ 1.
2.
3.

Name:_____ 1.
2.
3.

Supplies needed: 1.

2.

3.

4.

Interested Face

"Who Goes First?" Chart

1. _____

2. _____

3. _____

4. _____

5. _____

6. _____

Copy the Picture

Score Sheet 1

Name	1	2	3	4

Score Sheet 2

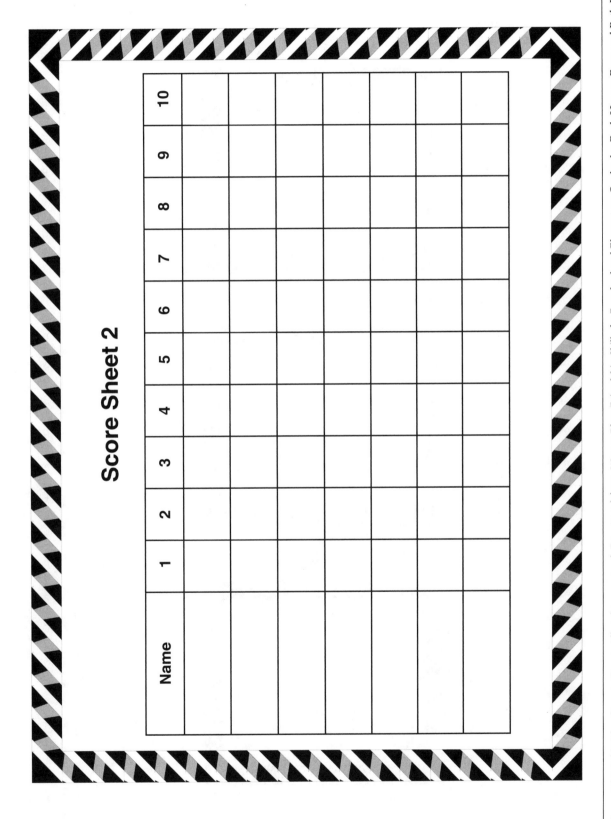

Name	1	2	3	4	5	6	7	8	9	10

What Happens Next?

**CORWIN
PRESS**

The Corwin Press logo—a raven striding across an open book—represents the union of courage and learning. Corwin Press is committed to improving education for all learners by publishing books and other professional development resources for those serving the field of PreK–12 education. By providing practical, hands-on materials, Corwin Press continues to carry out the promise of its motto: **"Helping Educators Do Their Work Better."**